Curveball: When Life Throws You a Brain Tumor

CURVEBALL

When Life Throws You a Brain Tumor

LIZ HOLZEMER

GHOST ROAD PRESS

Library of Congress Cataloging-in-Publication Data.
Ghost Road Press
Curveball: When Life Throws You a Brain Tumor
ISBN: 0978945670 (Trade Paperback)
Library of Congress Control Number: 2006935379

Printed in Canada.

Book Design: Sonya Unrein
Cover photo: Sandy Puc'

Ghost Road Press, Denver, Colorado
ghostroadpress.com

ACKNOWLEDGMENTS

It wasn't easy and for a time, I didn't know myself if this book would ever see a bookshelf. Thankfully, it did before my self-imposed fortieth birthday deadline.

I am grateful to the following team players:

Mark for being the one and for giving me the space and solitude to write when the juices were flowing.

Dr. Fullagar & Dr. Zager for putting my brain back together and tightening the ever-so-quirky bolts even more. I'm only here because of you both.

Mom, Dad, Elliot, Josh, and Jonathan for the encouragement I needed to reach the summit.

For Amber, Vivian, and Diva who knew the reason would eventually arrive, and for Marion and Nancy, my guardian angels.

My fantastic international Australian editing team—Lindy and Mel. I know there were many times both of you were grateful to be on the other side of the world during this laborious process.

Lindy—you believed when I didn't. I am eternally grateful for the Friday night editing sessions, DAM, and finally, what happens in Vegas, stays in Vegas. This far surpasses ASOE, now doesn't it?

GoTalk for the unbelievable calling plan.

Peter and Brad—yes, Miss America is calling again.

Lizzie and Jacinta at Epilepsy ACT in Canberra for your reassurance that we'd both be okay.

Matt Davis and Sonya Unrein at Ghost Road Press for getting my vision and for their unwavering enthusiasm.

My second family of mommas and poppas—finding all of you was better late than never.

My darlings who know when to let me rest and when to drag me out of the house to spontaneously embrace life. This is for you Hannah and Hunter.

As for me, I know of nothing else but miracles.
—Walt Whitman

For Hannah and Hunter

My miracle sweet pea and monkey, who saved my life.

PREFACE
PETER MCLAREN BLACK, M.D., PH.D.

This is a winning book about baseball, babies, and a brain tumor. As a journalist and the spouse of a professional baseball pitcher, Liz Holzemer found her world shattered by the discovery of a baseball-sized benign tumor—a meningioma—in her right temporal lobe. She describes her personal journey through the first unrecognized seizures, diagnosis of the tumor, surgery, postoperative recovery, further surgery, despair, long-awaited pregnancy, return of seizures, and finally a return to a vibrant, energetic life. The result is an authentic, funny book that is enormously readable. It ends with Liz's creation of Meningioma Mommas, an international organization with more than two thousand members whose goal is to teach and learn about meningiomas. This book demonstrates the reason that Liz has been given many awards for her courage and optimistic approach to life.

For doctors, this account provides a patient's reality to supplement our textbook phrases like "This tumor may present with a seizure" or "There may be subtle cognitive and emotional difficulties during recovery." Often as physicians and surgeons, we do not consider how devastating the disorders we deal with each day are in the daily lives of our patients.

For all readers, this book is an example of a particular kind of courage—one that uses inner strength; a supportive partner; good medical care; and friends to get through a difficult situation and emerge triumphant. The story has a happy ending, but it is not clear early on that this will be the case.

Ms. Holzemer is not alone in having a meningioma. You or I could suddenly be found to have one; its growth is often undetected until it is picked up following a seizure or on a scan done for another reason. Brain tumors in general are not well studied because they are not as common as lung, breast, prostate, or colon cancers; meningiomas have generally been ignored even more than other brain tumors. For many years they were not even included in cancer statistics, so we did not have an accurate idea of their incidence (how many new cases there are a year) or prevalence (how many people are alive with this kind of tumor). We now believe that a new meningioma is diagnosed in approximately one in a thousand people each year and that at least 138,000 people in the United States are living with a meningioma.

From research, we also are finding out more about these tumors. We know that meningiomas occur about twice as often in women as in men. We think that taking hormone replacement therapy makes it slightly more likely that you will get a meningioma. We know that some genetic disorders—most commonly neurofibromatosis—are associated with this tumor. We know that radiation can cause a meningioma twenty years later. We do not think cell phones or head trauma contribute to meningioma formation. We are getting better and better at identifying and removing a meningioma with microsurgery or image-guided minimally invasive surgery; and at using focused radiation as an adjunct or alternative to surgery.

There is much we still need to learn, however. Why do some of these tumors grow more aggressively than others?

What changes cause them in the first place? Can we develop animal or cell culture models of them so we understand better how to manage them? Could we begin to develop drugs that could keep them from progressing, or ways of placing therapies in a tumor at surgery to keep it from growing in the future? Can we use better imaging to follow their progression and know if they are likely to grow again? Will molecular biology help us to understand them better?

As a neurosurgeon working with patients with meningiomas almost daily, I hope that we will be able to answer these questions in the next few years. Groups like Meningioma Mommas are vitally important to accomplish this goal and to teach us all about these tumors. The Brain Science Foundation, which works closely with Meningioma Mommas, is a similar group. Through its Meningioma Project, it has the mission to enhance clinical care, research, and education in meningiomas. These organizations fill a real need because traditional brain tumor foundations and grant agencies concentrate on malignant brain tumors and tend to ignore meningiomas.

Liz Holzemer has done a great service to doctors and patients alike in writing this book. As a journalist, she has been able to capture the agony and joy of living through a brain tumor with sensitivity and humor. Read it to understand how an intelligent, gifted, life-loving woman survives hard medical times. I certainly hope that through this book and through Meningioma Mommas, Liz's influence will steadily grow to help meningioma patients everywhere.

Dr. Peter McLaren Black is Chair of the Department of Neurosurgery at Brigham and Women's Hospital, Boston; the Franc D. Ingraham Professor of Neurosurgery at Harvard Medical School; the Chief of Neurosurgical Oncology at the Dana Farber Cancer Institute; and is Neurosurgeon-in-Chief at Children's Hospital

"Life is like a baseball game. When you think a fastball is coming, you gotta be ready to hit the curve."—**Jaja Q**

INTRODUCTION

When I set out to write this book, it wasn't a matter of how to get started, but how to coherently commit my scattered thoughts to paper. As a writer, I had to give myself many allowances as my probed squishy gray matter slowly regained its shape. It took a long time for the misfiring neurons to make viable, sensible connections all over again. This story has been brewing since I reemerged from those double OR doors and became that unfamiliar Liz. I struggled, but during my brain tumor journey, I have rediscovered the voice that has at last made its way to print.

My goal for this book is to achieve three simple things:

1. Allay the fear that anchors and unites each of us who are living with a brain tumor sentence.

2. Quell the nightmares that jolt you awake in the dead of night, because few can grasp the private hell you will at times experience.

3. And finally, when the calm returns—because it *will*—provide you with a friend to whom you can turn and so embrace the love, laughter, and life that are yours now.

You've been granted a second chance—so live it.

CHAPTER ONE
OUT OF LEFT FIELD

The ball shall be a sphere formed by yarn wound around a
small core of cork, rubber or similar material...It shall weigh
no less than 5 nor more than 5 ¼ ounces and measure
no less than 9 nor more than 9 ¼ inches in circumference.
—**Official Rules of Major League Baseball**

I am more than familiar with this definition. My husband Mark,
a former major league ballplayer who pitched for fifteen seasons, spent a considerable amount of time manipulating that
five ounce sphere. As his wife, I've grown as comfortable rec-
ognizing its size and shape as he has, whether watching him
effortlessly throw a 90 m.p.h. fastball off the mound at the
formerly and appropriately called Angel Stadium in Anaheim,
California, or offering up a nasty slider from behind the rusty
chain link fences in Aragua, Venezuela.

So the irony wasn't lost on us when we learned I had something similarly sized growing inside of me. The shock however,
is still as palpable as it was that day I first heard four life-altering words.

Even though it was over seven years ago, I still can't shake
the memory and the overriding fear I had one February morning

when I fumbled for the phone before the sun had even risen.

"You have a meningioma," the voice on the other end stated gravely and evenly.

"A wh-what?" I stuttered.

"A *brain tumor*," the voice continued, sending chills down my spine.

"How do you even spell that?" I wanted to know as I desperately searched in my night stand drawer for a pen, a pencil—aw heck, a lip liner would do.

Men-in-gioma sounds more like a group of guys test-driving the latest foreign import with all the bells and whistles, not to mention the 8.9 percent available financing option.

If only it could have been that simple.

"Oh honey, what is it?" Mark asked, with the same fear registering across his face.

A flood of tears washed over me.

"I ha-have a brain tumor," I eked out. "A brain tumor with a funny name I don't even know how to say."

Mark fought to maintain his composure.

"I'm going to die," I cried harder.

"Honey, slow down, slow down," Mark tried reassuring me. "Let's just wait until we meet with the doctor and see how serious it is first. Try not to get all worked up."

How does a person *not* get all worked up over a brain tumor?

I took a long shower, turning the faucet until the water boiled. My limbs turned beet red. It didn't matter—I had no feeling.

I pulled on an old pair of jeans, gray turtleneck sweater, gray socks, and my blue and gray hiking boots. Gray to match the day and my mood. I resembled a TV commercial for clinical depression. The only difference being, there was no change in the before and after like on TV. I walked downstairs wondering, what do you even begin to ask a neurosurgeon?

Just a few hours later, Mark and I sat in horror as my newly appointed neurosurgeon translated my MRI. Never-before heard terms literally went over my head.

Middle third sphenoid wing meningioma.
Cavernous sinus.
Midline shift.
Lateral ventricular compression.

You'd have to be a brain surgeon to understand any of this stuff. Thankfully, Dr. Timothy Fullagar was.

Wait, I have a neurosurgeon?
A guy who works on brains for a living?
What was he going to do to mine?
He doesn't look much older than me!
Hang on, to get to my brain, he would have to…

I couldn't go there. I looked to Mark for comfort, but all he could do was grip my hand even tighter. His expression was as blank as mine felt.

I forced myself to look at the snapshots of my brain illuminated in Dr. Fullagar's office, shocked as the images of a baseball-sized mass (maybe it was a baseball?) glared back at me in defiance. The size and pressure of my tumor was so great that it had actually shifted my brain to its mid-line.

"You've probably had this tumor for over a decade," Dr. Fullagar continued in his monotone, neurosurgeon voice.

"A decade!" I had a "roommate" living inside of my head for ten years? The only roommates I ever recalled having back in college were the ones who shared their English lit notes with you and offered aspirin and a glass of water after a night of one too many beers.

There had to have been some sort of mix-up. A serious mistake. I couldn't get out of my head the *Kindergarten Cop* scene in which Arnold Schwarzenegger shouted, "It's not a tumor!" I so wanted to believe this. But this wasn't a movie.

It was real life and it was mine.

Our lives had been rudely interrupted by a brain tumor and the need to have brain surgery. *Brain. Surgery. Brain surgery.* My tongue fumbled each time Dr. Fullagar repeated, "Brain surgery is recommended as soon as possible."

If he hadn't already been booked—I thought you only booked dinner reservations or airline tickets—Dr. Fullagar would have operated the next day. He reminded Mark and me of the urgency of my situation.

His eyes shifted to Mark's. "Any longer, and you could have awakened one morning to discover that your wife had already slipped into a coma." Mark and I looked at each other with a chilling realization of what was at stake.

However, Dr. Fullagar did explain that if you were going to have a brain tumor—I don't ever recall this being a conscious choice on my part—a meningioma was the best kind to have.

My first crash course of the day—brain tumors. The not so bad, the bad, and the really bad. A meningioma is considered benign for the most part, as they grow on the meninges or outer lining of the brain, rather than attaching themselves to the brain. But in my case, since my meningioma had been growing for as long as ten years, it had time to get comfortable and used to its surroundings. Sort of like breaking in your favorite easy chair or pair of jeans.

Mine was affecting three critical areas—my optic nerve, carotid artery, and my sinus cavity. Surgery would be long and risky, but I didn't have a choice.

"Is it cancer?" I stammered.

"Can you remove it all?" Mark asked next.

Dr. Fullagar said my tumor wasn't cancer and that he was confident he could remove it all, but cautioned that he wouldn't really know until he was inside of my head.

Inside of my head. Those words penetrated me to the core.

Dr. Fullagar used a model of the brain to explain how he would evict the uninvited guest that had taken up residence. Neurosurgeon-speak continued to float over my head.

Surgical debulking.
Embolization.
Preoperative and postoperative seizure prophylaxis.

I had a feeling I'd soon be mastering a new foreign language. Meningioma had already been enough for one day.

Then came the second crash course—seizures. I had been experiencing unexplained "episodes," periodic moments of déjà vu or strange visions. Sometimes I'd see the color of leaves more vividly, or shoppers at Target would appear to suddenly speed up and zip in and out of the aisles, as if someone had pushed a fast forward button on life. These episodes only lasted twenty to thirty seconds, so I had discounted them.

Dr. Fullagar explained they were actually simple partial seizures and they were quite common in frontal lobe tumors. Seizures? Surely not. My understanding of seizures had been frothing at the mouth and uncontrollable convulsions.

Mark and I walked out of that office not saying a word—we knew each other well enough to know words would be of little comfort to either of us. We just didn't know where to begin.

In my hand, I carried instructions to admit myself to Swedish Medical Center seven days later, and a list of prescriptions to fill that were as troubling to comprehend as my diagnosis.

Dilantin—Three pills three times a day.
Decadron—4 mg four times a day with food.
Pepcid—to make eating even possible after taking the first two.

I hoped the Dilantin would control my seizures. I was to start this one immediately and would have to stay on the anti-seizure medication for at least six months after surgery, as a precaution. I gathered this was standard operating procedure in the *When You Have to Have Brain Surgery* manual.

Decadron is a steroid, which would stop my brain from swelling during surgery and I'd have to stay on it as well, but not nearly as long as the Dilantin. This must have also been in the manual.

I would now be popping pills round the clock. While Mark stopped off at our local Walgreens to fill my many prescriptions, the cliché *this happens to other people, not me* reverberated. My mind kept hitting the rewind button.

I had always considered myself healthy. I loved to hike and walk. I ate well. I couldn't possibly be harboring a life-threatening tumor if I could lead a normal lifestyle, could I?

I was only thirty-two at the time—too young, I thought, to have a tumor, let alone one growing in my head. Not only that, three years earlier—when Mark was pitching for the Seattle Mariners—I'd had a golf-ball sized fibroid adenoma removed from my left breast. My body must have a propensity for growing sports-themed equipment. Like a tumor minefield.

Mark and I had been trying to start a family for the past year. It had been five years since we exchanged our vows in front of a French minister at the Candlelight Wedding Chapel in Las Vegas. Our romance had an international and national flair—I was a Southern California gal; he a proud Colorado native. We had met in Vancouver through a mutual friend and a year later, eloped to Vegas after one of his on-the-road games. We were destined to be, as before we'd even met, I had enrolled in a journalism master's program at the University of Colorado at Boulder. Baseball had taken us to places I would not have otherwise experienced—Vancouver, Seattle, and three tours of Winter Ball duty in Aragua and Valencia, Venezuela, and Hermosillo, Mexico.

We were both in our early thirties. We had an empty home—save for our six-month-old yellow lab, Koufax—in a safe, suburban neighborhood. It was time to fill it with a son or daughter. At the start of spring training in 1999 while Mark was with the Oakland Athletics, I tossed my last packet of birth control pills. Whoosh! Down the toilet the pills went as a celebratory smile spread across my face.

My doctor had told me to expect irregular periods for several months as my body adjusted to being off the Pill. After all, I'd been on those white and brown placebo tablets for nearly a decade. I imagined it would take little time to become pregnant; weren't we constantly warned in high school how easy it was if we weren't careful?

On the last day of spring training, Mark was released from the Oakland Athletics. It was the worst time for a player to lose his job. Instead of starting a promising season in Oakland, we were taking a sixteen-hour drive back to Denver. As we wove our way through Albuquerque, Santa Fe, Pueblo, Trinidad, and Colorado Springs, the only way to reassure ourselves was to keep repeating, "There has to be a reason behind this." We wouldn't learn the eerie truth to this statement for almost another year.

While Mark's agent shopped for possible leads—which were very unlikely since every baseball team already had its roster set for Opening Day—we took advantage of our time together. "We have more chances to try for that family now!" I'd say enthusiastically.

April and May went by without a period or a positive pregnancy test. In June, Mark signed a minor league contract with the Colorado Rockies. It was the first time in his playing career that he could live in his own home and commute to the stadium. In this case, he'd be driving to Colorado Springs to pitch for the Sky Sox.

I couldn't help but think this was a sign that Mark was meant to be closer to home so we could become pregnant. What else could the reason be?

Even with Mark at home and me accompanying him on several road trips as I usually did every season, my body continued to fail me.

I found myself spending most of July and August either filling tubes with more blood samples or having my ob-gyn insist I call her by her first name. She ruled out thyroid problems, lupus, and other diseases. She even told me to reduce strenuous exercise and to increase my caloric intake.

"It certainly wouldn't hurt you to drink a McDonald's milkshake every day," I recall her saying. A prescription to gain weight—who would have thought?

Our hopes of starting a family evaporated as the days slipped by. It was time to kick things up a notch. I went through two cycles of fertility drugs in an attempt to jump-start my body into having periods. My body resisted. I became a raging hormonal maniac instead. I was temperamental, touchy, to be avoided. It was good timing Mark was on a seventeen-day road trip—the longest of the season.

I received an invitation to yet another baby shower. I was the only woman I knew whose mailbox was stuffed with more baby shower invites or announcements than junk mail. Meant to be celebrated, the painstakingly beautifully crafted announcements made me cry. Did I really need constant reminders of my failure to become a mom?

My doctor thought I was a good candidate for Clomid, which is often used to stimulate the release of multiple eggs. Still nothing.

Mark's season ended over Labor Day weekend. A few weeks later, his agent called and asked if he was interested in playing Winter Ball in Hermosillo, Mexico. Since Mark had a shortened season with fewer innings pitched than usual, we thought it would be a good opportunity for him to go. It would also improve his chances of signing with another team for the 2000 season.

I decided to stay back. I'd had my share of living out of suitcases over the seasons and had a great opportunity to assist a classroom of special needs kids at one of our local high schools. I thought it would shift the focus away from my worries.

But I was only kidding myself.

My ob-gyn had done all she could do too. In December 1999, she referred me to a fertility specialist, who diagnosed me with *hypothalamic hypogonadtrophism*. Translation—my ovulatory capacity had malfunctioned and prematurely shut down.

The unspoken fear I'd been harboring but didn't want to admit was staring me in the face.

He also said there was a possibility I had a non-cancerous pituitary tumor and in-vitro fertilization would be my only chance of becoming pregnant. I would have to take hormonal injections as part of my treatment. He cautioned there were no guarantees and it would be expensive.

I thought this was the worst news a doctor could ever deliver to a patient. Little did I know—

Mark's reaction to this latest obstacle thrown in our path was one of total support.

"Let's get through the holidays and then we'll start fresh," he said.

"That sounds like a game plan," I said. We decided to start treatment in January upon his return from Mexico.

It wouldn't be long before we'd be ushering in a new millennium. The birth of a new era and I couldn't get pregnant. I didn't even have viable eggs.

Mark hoped to fly home in time for Christmas. His team would have a few days off. It was the one time I wasn't rooting for his team to advance to the Winter Ball playoffs, but they did. He'd spend Christmas and New Year's in Mexico and I would join him in January if his team were still in contention.

I decided to fly home to California and spend the holidays

with my family and my college friend, Amber. It didn't take her long to notice that the Liz she knew from college wasn't the Liz she knew now.

"You're not your normal vibrant self," she observed, moments after my arrival at LAX.

As usual, I blamed it on the distance between Mark and me, focusing on trying to become pregnant, the holidays. But she wasn't fooled.

"It's something more," she said. "Take a look at yourself—you're dressed all in black and khaki. You look and act depressed."

"I can't help it, it's how I feel," I said defeated. "I just don't feel like me."

I'd been having excruciating headaches on a weekly basis. I heard swishing noises in my right ear when I went to bed and when I woke up. It sounded like my head was stuck in a washing machine or waves crashing on the beach. There were also the frequent déjà vu sensations. Again, I shrugged them off to stress.

"I have the perfect idea," Amber suggested the next day. "There's a huge New Year's Eve party next week. Let's go dance, have fun and celebrate. It might take your mind off everything."

"Go on without me," I said, knowing I was disappointing a well-meaning friend.

"Where's the Liz I know?" Amber cried. "The fun, hip, smart, stylish Liz, who loves adventures?"

I didn't know myself. Where had I disappeared to? Yes, it was out of character that I had no interest in celebrating the New Year. I only craved a quiet evening at home.

While lying in bed listening to the fireworks continue into the early hours of the millennium morning, I realized that Amber was right. There was something more. Everything began to add up and I started to question what my doctor had told me. My red flags were waving out of control—I'm a journalist; it's in my nature to investigate. There was a missing piece to the story and I was starting to believe *I* was that piece.

If in fact I did have a pituitary tumor, shouldn't this be ruled out before I started taking hormones? I couldn't rest easy without exploring the source of my increasing health problems.

It was January 2000. After an annual exam later that month, I told my ob-gyn that weekly hormonal injections didn't sit well with Mark or me. I was learning you have to be your own advocate and be vigilant about your health, especially if your instincts are hoisting up those red flags.

My doctors conferred and finally agreed to set up an MRI for me on the evening of February 2, 2000.

The last year of my life quickly finished playing. Now I watched Mark emerge from Walgreens with white, crinkly paper sacks, their contents designed to pave the way for my upcoming brain surgery. A life-threatening surgery to remove the tumor that had invaded my brain and my life.

CHAPTER TWO
STEP UP TO THE PLATE

Ya Gotta Believe!—**Tug McGraw**

Fear is only as deep as the mind allows.—**Japanese Proverb**

Shell-shocked. I now knew the true meaning of the word. As we arrived home, I kept repeating to myself, "Eight days, eight days." I had only eight days to prepare for brain surgery. This wasn't like preparing for one of Mark's road trips. I would do anything to be packing a smaller version of my closet for Tempe, Arizona, or California, or anywhere else for that matter. I needed warmth to soothe my chilled bones. Everything around me looked and felt devoid of color.

I wanted to hide. Run away. If only I could put enough miles between this brain tumor and me, I'd be safe. I hadn't even been granted a grace period to digest what we'd been told. Instead, I was faced with the daunting task of breaking the incomprehensible news to my friends and family.

But how the hell do you tell someone that you have a brain tumor and just hours ago you signed a piece of paper saying that you understood that you could go blind, suffer a stroke, become paralyzed, slip into a coma, or even die?

Would it become easier after the first call?

"Hi. Oh, um, hey guess what Mom and Dad? No, I'm not pregnant. Well, I do have something growing inside of me, but it's not your granddaughter or grandson. It's a ten-year-old brain tumor! No, I won't be registering at Babies R' Us or Target."

The real version went more along the lines of my misdialing a number my parents have had since I was born. My fingers eventually stopped shaking long enough for me to make a connection. As soon as my mom answered hello, the words just tumbled out of my mouth.

"Mom, I have a brain tumor and I'm having surgery in eight days," I said matter-of-factly, as if I were delivering the news on someone else's behalf. Oh how I wish that were the case; I would have done *anything* to be just the messenger.

There was an uncomfortably long pause on the other end.

"Oh dear, Liz," she finally said after processing the grim news for what seemed like an eternity. "I'll be there for surgery and stay as long as you need me."

I was so thankful that she offered to call my three younger brothers and my aunt for me. I never thought having a small extended family would ever prove beneficial. I didn't have many relatives to share the dreadful news with.

Mark, on the other hand, had extended family throughout Colorado, North Dakota, and Minnesota, so he made those calls while I figured out exactly when I was supposed to take each pill, if I could take them together, and how long I had to wait before eating. It was overwhelming and confusing. I lined up my varying-sized vials next to my vitamins on the kitchen counter. Now my brain tumor was taking over my house as well.

As relatives relayed the message, we were inundated with calls expressing concern and offering comfort. The expected questions followed:

What kind of brain tumor? Does it really matter?
How did this happen? How the hell do I know?
When did you find out? You're one of the first to know.
When is surgery? Too soon.

What can we do? I have no idea; this is all new territory for us too.

It would have been much easier to leave a recording on our answering machine: *Liz has a brain tumor. Supposedly, it's the good kind to have. How's this for irony—it's as big as a baseball. She's having surgery in eight days. We are just as dazed and confused as you are and don't have any answers. Please pray for us and keep us in your thoughts. Thank you.*

I couldn't breathe. I had to step outside to collect myself.

My next-door-neighbor, Vivienne, was walking up the drive with a bouquet of purple irises in her hand. Vivienne had only moved in four months ago, yet we had clicked instantly. Her South African accent won me over the first time she introduced herself.

I had no idea how much I needed her warm embrace, and at first, words weren't necessary. I don't remember how long I shook in her arms, my heart heaving. We sobbed together and I could barely make out Vivi's muffled words.

"Oh Lizzy," she said. "What are we going to do about this?"

Everyone should have a friend like Vivi—she instantly took on her friends' problems. She didn't believe in their tackling them alone.

"Come," she insisted, as I followed her next door. That was our signal for *There's nothing like a cup of soothing tea and decadent chocolates* to solve another one of life's curveballs. However, I knew no amount of mandarin orange spice tea and Belgium chocolates would soften the shock.

"At least while recovering you'll have an excuse to wear the latest spring fashion in hats," Vivi said tearfully, trying to cheer me up.

For all her good intentions, her comment had the opposite effect. The thought hadn't crossed my mind to ask Dr. Fullagar about my head being shaved. I think I was preoccupied rereading the "could be blind, paralyzed, slip into a coma/die clause." I know it sounds vain, but now it was like a double whammy, not only was I going to have brain surgery, I'd be bald.

A ridiculous thought popped into my head—I'd only recently indulged in hi-lights and a haircut. What a shame. Did my hairdresser have a refund policy for emergency brain surgery? I'd have to remind myself to check.

Shaved. Bald. Like Barry Bonds.

I wasn't going to look like Demi Moore in *G.I. Jane,* that was for sure.

At least I still had some semblance of my sense of humor. Oh God, what would happen upstairs while Dr. Fullagar removed my tumor? He did say it would be a lengthy and risky surgery. What if he accidentally scraped off one too many neurons or tampered with the part of my brain that gave me the ability to write, be creative, be me.

Okay, slow down Liz. Where is your tumor? On the right side. So the right side controls the left side. Oh, this was all too much. I needed to leave Vivi's and conduct some research of my own.

Internet search: Meningeeohma. Nothing. Menangmoa. Nothing.

"Fuck, how the hell do you spell this damn thing?" I shouted from our study.

I gave up in frustration and just typed in brain tumor. Pages and pages of links filled my screen. Where should I start? I wished the reason for my frantic Internet search were to merely look up a recipe. You know, three ingredient dinners or no cooking desserts.

Well, I quickly learned that I wasn't alone. Nearly 190,000 people would hear the life shattering words *you have a brain tumor* this year.

In a panic, I clicked away on website after website. Brain tumor after brain tumor with names as difficult to pronounce as mine were listed casually, like you were ordering from McDonald's—fries with that? Sundae? Super-size your meal?

Detailed color diagrams and pictures filled my monitor. Now we're talking! The images were graphic. These websites should have a disclaimer: *Don't read if you've been recently diagnosed or, for that matter, have ever had a brain tumor unless you want to be scared out of your mind.* Maybe a rating system like the movies would work. No G, PG, PG-13, or R-ratings here. It was x-rated all the way.

And there were various treatment options with fancy names to match—gamma knife, CyberKnife, radiosurgery—I was drowning in a sea of information overload, desperately searching for a lifeline.

But it didn't end. Dictionary definitions of chemotherapy, malignant, atypical, reoccurrence. I didn't have cancer or did I? One site said meningioma had a fifteen to twenty percent chance of growing back. Although I was never fond of math, I knew enough that this meant one out of every five with a meningioma, at some point in their life, would have to lay out the welcome mat again.

Another website even had an "In Memoriam" page. My heart raced. I had no idea how many famous people had died from a brain tumor—Lee Atwater, George Gershwin, Tim Gullikson, Bob Marley, Ethel Merman, Gene Siskel, Dan Quisenberry—

Most were quite young—like me.

The next stats froze every muscle in my body. They leapt out of the screen stating I had a poorer chance of survival than a breast cancer patient did. How could that be? I have a "good" brain tumor don't I? I was already a breast tumor survivor. Now I had a brain tumor. Would having both shave significant years off my life?

Yet, I kept scrolling down. I thought I had read it all until I found detailed descriptions on what was actually involved during surgery, or *craniotomy,* as it's correctly called. The sound of that word alone raised every hair on my body. It sounded so barbaric. The image of Jack Nicholson's character, Randle Patrick McMurphy, undergoing a frontal lobotomy in *One Flew over the Cuckoo's Nest,* popped into my head. I did have a right frontal lobe meningioma. Surgeons didn't perform frontal lobotomies anymore, did they?

Suddenly, I felt queasy and light-headed. Did I really need to know what kind of saw or size blade Dr. Fullagar would use to carve open my skull? Or that he would pull back my bone flap, remove a part of my skull to create a "window" to access my tumor and then screw it all back together like the Bride of Frankenstein?

This wasn't the helpful information I was looking for. I hadn't thought it was possible, but I was even more terrified than before. I needed to talk to someone with a meningioma, or any other type of brain tumor. I didn't want the graphic and gory details. I wanted to be face to face with a survivor. Anyone who was living proof that he or she had survived brain surgery, proving that I could, too. Was there life after a brain tumor and if so, what was it like? So many questions. Could I find the answers I needed in eight days? I doubted it.

Instead, I shifted my focus to what I could control—spending as much time with Mark as possible. With the exception of the few hours he needed every day to work out and throw to get his arm ready for spring training, we were inseparable.

Mark did his best to occupy my mind with anything other than my upstairs roommate. We dined at our favorite Mexican restaurant a few times even though the food was tasteless to me. Great, I couldn't even enjoy the extra spicy salsa or the green-chile-covered carne asada burritos. Were the medications dulling my senses or was the impending surgery casting its somber shadow over my mood?

Mark also took me shopping to buy new walking shoes and a few warm up suits. We'd be facing the snowiest month of the season in Colorado—March—and I'd still be in the early weeks of my recovery.

"I think you'll be more comfortable in these," he said lovingly, as he pulled another navy blue Nike sweat suit from the racks.

"Seems like a lot of money to spend for a depressing hospital," I mumbled. "And it's not like I'll be training for a marathon."

"Could you stop being so damn practical," Mark replied, exasperated. "I want you to feel good."

I hadn't even thought about recovery yet. I most feared losing my ability to write, but would I also have physical deficits? What if I couldn't even button or unbutton a blouse; zip up a pair of jeans? Would I lose control of my own hands?

Once my post-surgery wardrobe was paid for, we went in search for new luggage for Mark. He had signed a contract with the Philadelphia Phillies, which turned out to be a strange blessing in disguise. In previous seasons, Mark had been extended a big league camp invite, which meant he was always spending Valentine's Day getting to know his new teammates, instead of spending time with his wife. This year he wouldn't leave for camp in Clearwater, Florida until March 1.

I wished it were me leaving. Instead, I had an upcoming date with blue-masked doctors and surgical equipment I dared not think about, followed by a new life to begin, if I survived. I only had days to say good-bye to myself. It wasn't very much time to prepare. I was thankful every morning I woke up, well aware the medications were keeping my brain from swelling or having seizures.

I wasn't up for visitors and luckily family wasn't arriving until either the day of surgery or afterwards. Mark and I had agreed I would need the greatest help during my recovery, and it made no sense sitting around discussing my impending fate.

Hey Liz, if you knew you only had eight days to live, how would you spend them?

I would take a Carvedless Cranium Carnival Cruise far, far away.

What's the one place you would love to see before you die?

Not a neuro ICU ward, that's for sure.

How would you like people to remember you?

Blonde, but not brain impaired.

This really wasn't the game I wanted to play.

A few days before my scheduled surgery, I returned to Swedish Medical Center for a full medical work-up and an appointment with Dr. Wayne Yakes, a world renowned interventional neuroradiologist. Why is it any term dealing with the brain is impossible to pronounce? Based on my tumor's size, I was told I had to have something called a cerebral angiogram and a pre-operative embolization. Sounded more like a strange embalming process to me.

Dr. Wayne Yakes was very kind and took his time explaining the upcoming procedures with Mark and me. Another crash course—*Surgery before Brain Surgery.* We had learned from his assistant that Dr. Yakes performed life saving miracles with only a few tools—wire as thin as fishing line, steady hands, and compassion as big as his heart. An atlas hung in his office decorated with a rainbow of pushpins—each one representing a state or country his talents had taken him to.

February 10, 2000, dawned all too soon, the day when I'd check in for my embolization prior to my surgery that was scheduled for the following day. I had a few more things to pack in my duffle bag. It was the same one I'd used for many road trips, the last one being to California when I visited my family and Amber. It had been packed with Hanukkah presents, sunscreen, and pictures Amber and I had snapped together.

The irony wasn't lost on me that my trip home had triggered the same alarm bells in my loved ones' heads that had resonated in my own. As a result, I was packing neatly folded sweat suits, walking shoes, a few toiletries and for good luck—a heart-shaped necklace Mark had given me on our first wedding anniversary.

I surveyed my house one final time in case its contents would look altered when I'd return. I had a deep sense that the next time I walked through the front door, I would be a different Liz than the one who had left.

Within an hour of our arrival at the hospital, I was prepped for the angiogram and embolization.

Dr. Yakes spent several hours threading a wire the width of floss from the right side of my groin up to the brain. If successful, the procedure would cut off the tumor's blood supply. Apparently, I had a vascular, blood-thirsty tumor, one whose appetite could create serious complications during surgery if it weren't placed on house arrest.

When I came to in ICU, a male nurse with kind eyes and an accent that was hard to instantly place, informed Mark and me that the procedure was successful.

He then introduced himself. "I'm Martin and I'll be caring for you over the next few days."

Thinking that he was Irish, I mustered up the energy to volunteer, "I backpacked through Ireland many years ago."

"Yes, Ireland is a lovely country, but Scotland's my home," he corrected me with a wink. "No worries, I'll still keep a watchful eye over you."

I couldn't pinpoint why, but Martin made me feel it would be okay and I *would* get through this.

I encouraged Mark to go home because I knew tomorrow would be more of a strain on him than on me. After all, I'd be knocked out. He assured me he would be there the next morning before I was wheeled away.

On the morning of surgery, I awakened to sunshine spilling into my ICU room. I still felt fuzzy from the anesthesia, yet I sensed a figure sitting beside me, the outline was indiscernible, but I knew it was a familiar face.

Then the voice and the touch of a warm hand made it all clear. My girlfriend Christi from Phoenix. Christi and her husband RJ had become our surrogate family years ago. RJ had employed Mark at the car dealership he worked for during the 1995 baseball strike. We were newlyweds, Mark's pitching days were on hold, and we were living in an apartment in Tempe, Arizona. While Mark tried his hand at selling American cars, I finished writing my Master's thesis.

What was Christi doing here?

"I just flew in this morning," she said, warming up my chilled hands. "I promised myself I wouldn't leave until I saw you safely emerge from surgery."

Family and friends were slowly gathering outside, each taking turns to briefly visit with me and share their well wishes. All too soon we had to say good-bye. They enveloped me with their love while holding hands and reciting the *Lord's Prayer*.

I couldn't help but feel that everyone was preparing for the worst as they finished with, "For thine is the kingdom, and the power, and the glory, for ever and ever. Amen."

My mother hung back after the circle broke up.

"Today, you've got a big mountain to climb," she said. "All you have to do is get to the summit."

My mom kissed my forehead and quickly turned, hoping to hide the tears that I already sensed were spilling down her face.

And then it was time. Martin announced they were ready for me on the ninth floor.

Another nurse joined him as they rolled me down the long impersonal, cold, white hallways. Mark kept up with their fast clip, still managing to hide his fear from me.

I was prepped for a stealth MRI, which would provide 3-D images of my brain and accurately guide Dr. Fullagar during surgery. A middle-aged technician explained how she was going to apply cool gel to my scalp and strategically attach what resembled green Cheerios. I imagined I would look like a map for a treasure hunt. 'X' marks the spot. Would they take a black Sharpie and mark the right side of my head—Enter Here!? I'd read about botched surgeries where doctors had removed the wrong organ or lopped off the wrong limb.

Surgery was delayed for what felt like an interminable amount of time—six hours in fact. As I lay on the gurney facing those stark and intimidating double steel doors, I couldn't help but think they represented the gateway to my new life. Finally, my anesthesiologist approached.

"Liz, I promise you are not going to feel a thing," he assured me. "I want you to think of your favorite place on the planet. That's where you're going for the rest of the day."

That was easy.

Shaw's Cove in Laguna Beach, California.

I'd spent every summer there for as long as I could remember. Images flashed—my mother hefting a picnic basket packed with her signature cream cheese and olive sandwiches, too-salty potato chips, and a jug of pink lemonade; my three younger brothers and me traipsing behind trying to keep up; mismatched beach towels and sand pails; a romantic walk along the shore with my first true love, admiring the burnt orange sun as it tucked itself into bed for the evening; and countless days spent alone scribbling in my sea-stained journal. It's where I wanted my cremated ashes dispersed. I hoped not yet.

Mark and I only had a few more moments together. Our fear had become palpable. His eyes communicated a sense of terror so intense I forced myself to look away. Mark had lost the most important woman in his life—his mother—to breast cancer when he was only ten. I felt tremendous guilt for putting him through this ordeal. Although we had refused to acknowledge it, surely the thought of losing his wife had crossed his mind.

"The next time you're in a hospital, I promise it will be to give birth to our son or daughter," he said confidently.

I managed a weak smile.

"I love you," he said, his voice cracking.

I reached for his hand and pumped it three times—it was our signal for "I love you."

"Bye hun," I cried. It was all I could manage; anything more and I would have broken down.

He said he'd be waiting to say hello to me again when it was all over.

My last conscious thought was burying my toes in the cool, familiar sand.

CHAPTER THREE
GOING, GOING, GONE

Looking at the ball going over the fence isn't going
to help.—**Hank Aaron**

If you woke up breathing, congratulations! You have another
chance.—**Andrea Boydston**

The real glory is being knocked to your knees and then
coming back. That's real glory.—**Vince Lombardi**

My first conscious moment was one of absolute horror. Tears
stung my eyes as the reality of what had happened hit me
hard. *Oh God, I've had brain surgery to remove a tumor.* The
tears continued, hot and prickly, tasting of brine. I was alone
and the only thing that separated me from the life I'd once
known and participated in was a thin, yellowing pair of drapes
on a metal rod.

I'd been reduced to gauze, bandages, and a trio of IV drips.
The cottage cheese ceiling above me inched closer and closer.
My heart pounded. I had the sensation you get when you have
that dream about plunging off a cliff or rolling down a mountain side. The dream when you wake up breathlessly on the
edge of your bed. You realize the drop is only two feet instead

of two thousand, and you half shake your head in amusement—and relief. I tried to move, but fear had immobilized me. Maybe I'd been angled a particular way as a post-op precaution not to ooze brain matter. Was this standard practice?

A parade of white coats moved hurriedly past me. In tow were murmuring voices.

"Pulse is good."

"Morphine drip started."

"Patient is stable."

I wasn't quite sure to whom the voices belonged, but I knew that I desperately needed something to quell the fiery, raw sensations in my throat.

"How are you feeling young lady?" a voice asked.

Just inches from my face were a pair of kind eyes I grappled to remember.

Scottish accent. Nice smile.

"Martin!" I gasped, wincing in pain—pain that wasn't nearly as bad as I'd expected because it was well managed by the morphine. Hopefully, it would stay that way.

I was swathed in overly starched sheets; a maze of tubes extended from my arms to a lifeline of various intimidating machines. Their intermittent bleeps and chimes gave me pause. Was I breathing on my own or was my pulse controlled by an inanimate object?

"You did marvelous," Martin said, answering my unspoken question as he dropped another ice chip into my mouth. The coolness was a welcome relief to my parched throat.

The vise grip on my heart eased. Color gradually returned to my whitened knuckles.

"Now move your toes," another familiar voice commanded.

It was Dr. Fullagar. Could I move my toes?

"Excellent," he said. Apparently I could.

"How many fingers," he continued, waving them in my direction.

"Three," I responded like an army recruit obeying her commander.

"I'll see you tomorrow," Dr. Fullagar said before turning around. "There's someone who's been waiting all night to see you."

"Hello hun," Mark said tearfully. "Thank God, you're alright. The doctor thinks he got it all."

Mark carefully navigated around the maze of tubes for an overdue embrace.

"I love you, I love you, I love you," the words gushed out. I was alive. Mark was here. It didn't seem possible, but it was.

"There's a waiting room full of people who want to see you," he said wearily.

"Only a few visitors at a time," Martin quickly interjected. "And it has to be brief. We don't want to raise her blood pressure through the roof," he added, placing a protective hand over mine.

My mom came in first.

"You made it to the summit," she said.

I nodded back. She was right—I had.

"What do you need?" she asked.

"Just hold my hand," I said.

And she did, sitting next to me, gently stroking it.

Family and friends continued filing in one by one and were politely asked to leave after a few minutes. My day had begun at sunrise and, with my surgery pushed back several times, midnight was quickly approaching.

Even though I'd been asleep for most of the day, I wanted nothing more than to close my eyes and put the nightmare behind me. I wanted to shut everything out. Brain surgery. Make it go away. Could the words brain and surgery be permanently erased from my mind? The same way you forget to save an important file on your hard drive? Like the time I'd accidentally lost the second version of my Master's thesis. This was the one time I wanted to erase my hard drive. *Tabula rasa.*

When I woke the next morning—my first morning as Liz, Brain Tumor Survivor—I remembered everything. My mental slate had an imaginary list of questions I was too afraid to ask.

Did they really get the entire tumor?
If not, what then?
How soon would I know?
How did they put my skull back together—Crazy Glue?
Screws? Industrial strength rubber cement?
Did I still look like me?

My thoughts were interrupted by raucous laughter. What on earth? Another voice chuckled. Then another. What was so damn funny? It sounded like a *Hee Haw* family reunion was unfolding just beyond the yellowed curtain. It took a few more unsettling moments for it to register that I'd been moved from the Neuro ICU to a different room. And I had a fucking roommate. God, yesterday, doctors had painstakingly evicted my decade-old upstairs roommate, and now I had more intruders? I don't recall this being in my *What to Expect the Day After Brain Surgery* manual. The last thing I thought I'd have to worry about was sharing my recovery room. Maybe if I'd had arm surgery, but this was my *brain*. A brain that had been mercilessly assaulted by pronged instruments and titanium bolts and screws, like shrapnel after the attack.

Then I heard my mother's voice booming like a sergeant's and dispensing orders.

"This is too Goddamn noisy!" she admonished. "My daughter has just had brain surgery. She can't stay here."

My mother's decades of nursing kicked into overdrive—she took control of the floor as if it were her own. There was no way in hell—no way—that one of her patients would have a roommate on *her* shift.

I must have looked visibly upset to her. I angled my head to the left and swallowed hard. "Wh-what's going on?" I asked.

"I've taken care of it," she assured me.

The nurse on duty reassured my mother and me that a private room would soon be available. I felt like a hotel guest who'd checked in too early only to be told my room hadn't yet been cleaned or restocked with fresh towels, useless one-portion-only sized shampoos, and body lotions. I didn't care about a newly made bed of hospital-issue itchy sheets and a climate controlled room. I just wanted out of here.

A few hours later, after my mom's persistence, I was finally moved to a private room. One would think that a cracked cranium would entitle you to a view of the Colorado Rockies, but instead my outlook was a pair of non-descript medical buildings. It didn't matter though. It was February. Gray. Bleak. Somber. Just like me.

The only thing I felt even remotely interested in was food. Who knew that brain surgery caused ravenous hunger pangs? My hadn't-been-fed-in-eighteen-hours gaunt frame—which my mother lovingly pointed out resembled the latest museum skeletal exhibit—craved food. I had visions of fluffy mashed potatoes, perfectly grilled and seasoned rib-eye steaks, and crisp asparagus enticing my palette. Brewed sun tea with a sprig of mint leaf washing it down. And the wafting aroma of just-out-of-the-oven peach cobbler adorned in quickly melting homemade vanilla ice cream was almost palpable. This summer vision warmed my legs, which, despite being dressed in thick elastic stockings to prevent blood clots, were ice cold.

My daydream was rudely interrupted by the overworked twenty-four-hour shift nurse slapping down a plate of slop in front of me, along with a paper Dixie cup full of tepid water to swallow another batch of pills. Mystery meat buried in watery gravy was supposed to bring me restorative powers and heal me? I hardly thought so. The obviously still-thawing vegetables were rubbery and tasteless. A stale wheat roll begging to find a home would remain homeless. The lemon meringue pie looked artificial and equally as rubbery as the green beans and carrots.

I reluctantly ate while holding my breath. I remember being told as a child by my mother and father that if you held your breath while eating something unappetizing, you wouldn't taste it going down. Well, they sugarcoated the truth. I begged Mark to bring me Dairy Queen German Chocolate Cake blizzards—one of my favorite desserts. Thankfully, too, Amber brought me her signature chicken and rice casseroles. My appetite increased and I couldn't understand why. Surely, I wasn't exerting much energy beyond daily leg exercises, which I performed in bed. I soon learned that the Decadron was responsible for my voracious appetite.

Several days passed in a blur of family visits and nurses disturbing the little sleep I managed with vital sign checking and catheter changing. Doctors appeared briefly, marking their obligatory clip-boarded charts that the "patient showed visible signs of life."

Finally, I had the opportunity and the courage to ask Dr. Fullagar what I desperately needed to confirm.

"Did you, were you...?" I stammered.

"I'm confident it was a full resection," he reassured me.

But how did he know for certain I wondered? I needed proof. Did he have it in a jar above his office labeled, "*World's Largest Big Ass Tumor*" or did he have it enclosed in a glass display case with all the rest of his trophy tumors, like Mark's collection of autographed baseballs in our basement. *Cal Ripken Jr. Derek Jeter. Roger Clemens. Liz Holzemer. Patient X. Patient Y.* And how old was it? Did it have symmetrical rings on it like those of a large Oak or Redwood? Realistically, I knew there were no guarantees.

My highly coveted private room quickly became a storage warehouse for heart-shaped foil balloons and floral arrangements. A poster had been tacked up with well wishes for a speedy recovery.

Mark surprised me with roses and chocolates on Valentine's Day.

"This is the worst Valentine's Day ever," I broke down sobbing. "I would do anything to be in Arizona for spring training right now."

"I would too," Mark agreed, in tears as well.

"I'm sorry honey," I kept on crying. "I appreciate everything you're doing."

"I know you do," Mark said.

I'd never felt so unromantic or unattractive in my life. That damn cupid hadn't smitten me with love, but rather, had impaled my heart and spirit with one too many arrows. And now that the heavy-duty anesthesia and morphine had all but evaporated, it felt like my cranium had been repeatedly clobbered with a two-by-four.

Maybe washing my hair would make me feel half-human again. Not only did I want to wash away any remnants of brain surgery, I was curious about what lurked beneath the swathe of gauze bandages. I was ready to confront the graphic evidence of what had been done to me.

"I'm ready!" I announced with false bravado, prepared to face the enemy. A nurse gently peeled off the days' old bandages.

"What if water gets into my head?" I couldn't help but ask.

"Don't worry, you're stapled shut!" the nurse assured me. The image of Dr. Fullagar's blue scrubbed-clad assistants bustling around with a staple gun, like construction workers finishing up another suburban tract neighborhood, sprung to mind.

Mark steadied me with his hands and walked me into the unforgiving light of the bathroom. Now I could finally witness firsthand physical proof that I'd survived brain surgery. That my roommate, which had overstayed its welcome, had been served a final eviction notice.

I braced myself for what I was about to see for the first time. I gripped the cold porcelain sink, drew in a deep breath, and hesitantly looked up.

I wasn't prepared for what I saw. My scalp hadn't been entirely shaved after all. And what remained of my hair was a sticky mess of dried blood and Betadyne. My face had a yellow-green pallor and my right eye had begun to swell shut. It looked like an army of wasps had established a new zip code across my entire face with their deadly venom. Then I slowly turned my head to the left—my fair-skinned head resembled a one-sided Mohawk without the spiked fringe on top.

I carefully touched my exposed scalp and traced the staples, which began above my right eye and extended to below my earlobe, resembling an upside down question mark. I lost count after forty.

"I look awful!" I shrieked.

"Liz, it's only been a few days," Mark said, still steadying me.

Once again, the magnitude of what had actually transpired hit home. Eleven days ago, I was living life as Liz Holzemer— healthy, early thirties, happily married baseball wife, freelance writer, just trying to fulfill my dreams of becoming a mother. But four words had completely altered the course of my life and now *this* rude awakening: looking at the new me, battered and bruised.

I felt myself losing consciousness and it was only Mark's protective embrace that prevented me from collapsing heavily against the linoleum. Between Mark and a nurse, I was hoisted back into my narrow bed. We'd postpone my first hair washing venture for another time. Besides, what did I really expect to achieve by washing half a head?

Six days after surgery, I was cleared to leave the hospital. As much as I wanted to go home, I didn't feel ready to relinquish the security of having help just a buzzer away. What if my staples opened up and brain oozed out? What if I started having seizures again? What if?

"You're going to do just fine," Dr. Fullagar assured me, before leaving detailed instructions on what I could and could not do for the next few weeks.

As I left my room, a prepped patient was wheeled past with the same look of paralyzing fear I had felt only days before. Her journey was beginning, while mine as a survivor was just unfolding. I was on my way to my new life.

CHAPTER FOUR
IT AIN'T OVER 'TIL IT'S OVER

You start chasing a ball and your brain immediately
commands your body to run forward! Bend! Scoop
up the ball! Peg it to first! Then your body says who me?
—Joe DiMaggio

Why did a road I'd traveled countless times feel so unfamiliar
and overwhelming? Maybe the images of dimly lit storefronts
and rapidly changing turn signals were too much for my freshly
probed and pummeled brain to process.

I recognized the intersections along Broadway, but it still felt
different. South on Broadway past "antique row," block after
block of car dealerships—some with older models boasting
their slashed prices in fluorescent numbers across windshields,
and others filled with the latest freshly waxed German and
Japanese models. Still south until the car lots gave way to
strategically placed strip malls adjacent from each other, mir-
roring the other's contents—bank, dry cleaner, fast food drive
thru, nail/hair/tanning salon. Then, Aspen and pine trees neatly
planted every few feet as we drove into our master planned
bubble of recreation centers, more strip malls, and cookie-
cutter homes painted in the required shades of blues, browns,
grays, and greens.

I felt excluded from these scenes. I wanted to reach out and touch them. Feel them. Were they real? Normal? If this was my life it was wrought with uncertainty and fear. Would I always feel this way?

A young mother bundled up in fleece pushed a stroller with an infant swaddled in receiving blankets. A couple turned onto a popular dirt trail path with a pair of hyper dogs—one a chocolate lab, the other a copper shaded retriever. A mailman stuffed bills and magazines into shiny metal boxes on a street corner.

And then we pulled into the driveway.

"We're home," Mark announced.

"I'm not sure what that's going to feel like," I said glumly.

I braced myself for what was behind the front door—a door that protected the contents of the life I had left only a week ago. A spring-like aroma wafting through the air greeted me. Fresh and inviting unlike the hospital smells of cafeteria food and Pine-Sol I'd been breathing.

I entered what resembled a florist shop rather than my own home. Freshly filled vases of stunning arrangements took over every corner. Dozens of red, white, and yellow roses waiting with anticipation to bloom, had been carefully placed around the living room and entry. Gerbera daisies—my favorite—in brilliant hues of yellow, orange, and fuchsia occupied a spot in the kitchen. Mylar balloons with messages shouting *Welcome Home! Happy Valentine's Day!* and *Get Well.* Cards lined the dining room table; an unopened stack filled a wicker basket, and messages blinked at me from the answering machine.

My eyes welled up from the numerous gestures of kindness from so many people. It was truly overwhelming.

Mark had made our couch into a bed with soft blankets and pillows, which Koufax was already warming up for me. A TV tray had everything I needed within reach—water, meds, lip balm, magazines, remote control, and cordless phone.

"Oh hun," I cried. "You thought of everything."

"Why don't you rest?" Mark offered. "You don't want to overdo it."

"No thanks," I said.

I'd been immobilized for the past week, I wanted to explore and rediscover my home. Could I still do the same things? How would things feel—running water on my hands, flannel sheets against my skin, cool tiles under my bare feet?

Everything was the same except for the two charts that had been taped to the refrigerator.

One read: *Meds Schedule*

Mark had taken a black Sharpie and drawn boxes after each medication—my new best friends—I was required to take. The chart was broken down into times of day and the dosage, to mark off upon completion.

The other: Liz Caretaker/Watch Dog Calendar, as if I were on house arrest. This chart was graphed out over the next three months with the names of family and friends who would stay with me. It reminded me of the time my parents took a trip and left detailed instructions for the hapless sitter watching over my three younger brothers and me. Would I have a curfew? Not allowed sugar past seven? And speaking of sugar, where was the weekly menu with each day's selections neatly typed out?

No sooner had I thought this when there was a knock at the door. Neighbors had come together to ensure Mark and I wouldn't starve over the coming weeks; this was the first delivery of many homemade meals.

My first culinary delight since the hospital hash was Italian fare. I hardly knew where to start. I anticipated the savory taste of homemade lasagna, the mozzarella still bubbling, when a shocking sensation knocked me back. My jaw muscles tightened up as if the right side of my face had been tacked behind my ear like a botched facelift. I tried another forkful. My jaw buzzed at me. Taut tension. Had a few of my facial nerves been accidentally nicked? It certainly felt like it. I angled my fork sideways. No improvement. The *What to Expect After Brain Surgery* manual hadn't prepared me for this either. Maybe I was expecting too much.

With the struggle of eating dinner over, my next hurdle was tackling the stairs so I could go to bed. I'd been told to carefully approach them like a hiker plotting out her map for the upcoming peak. Easy as pie I thought as I began my trek up the low pile Berber carpet. I'd done plenty of hiking in my lifetime since my mom first introduced me to Mount Ritter and Lake Ediza in the High Sierras. Why then, halfway up, did I suddenly feel like my legs could buckle without warning? Lead weight forced me to slow down. Grip the banister. Chin up. Target in sight. I bit down on my lip as I mustered up the strength to lift my feet, which felt like bags of cement.

"Just a few more stairs," I kept thinking to myself, as I ascended stair after stair until I'd made it. "I did it!"

I savored my victory as I finally collapsed into bed.

I awoke the next morning determined to achieve another victory. My dizzy spell in the hospital had prevented me from completing something of utmost importance—my first post-op shampoo. Fortunately, we had a deep kitchen sink with an extended faucet. I propped myself up on our kitchen counter and angled my legs across the stove. What a sight. Mark folded several towels under my neck and had me lean back while he carefully sprayed warm water over my scalp.

"I can almost imagine being at the salon," I teased him.

"Just call me Jose Eber," Mark joked. "I wills makes you zee beautiful."

In bliss, I felt the week's worth layers of Betadyne disappearing. Better still, I didn't feel any water leaking into my head—so far so good! Forty-five minutes later with my energy tapped out, it was back to the couch—my sanctuary.

My days were divided into perfectly orchestrated chunks of time dictated by my medication schedule or the need to satiate my Decadron-fueled appetite. Once I had carefully navigated my way down the stairs, I would spend the rest of the day ensconced on the couch. The only relief from the tedium was meal breaks and the prescribed one-lap shuffle around the block, which drained my always-near-empty energy reservoir.

My mom stayed with me for two weeks and became the self-appointed rest regulator. She happily took over the job of keeping visitors at bay.

"They're gone," she said again one afternoon.

"Mom, you don't have to shoo off all visitors," I groaned.

"You don't need to expend all your energy on trying to visit and make small talk," she explained. "I feel like your protector and I have no problem doing it."

As the swelling subsided, the pain level increased. Newton's Third Law—*for every action, there is an equal and opposite reaction*—took on a whole new meaning. My numb nerves were awakening like anesthesia wearing off after a root canal, and it was excruciating. Consequently, sleep proved elusive. How on earth was I ever going to heal if I couldn't sleep, I agonized? I had Vicodin for the pain, which was also the only thing that knocked me out for a few hours. The downside was how dangerous it could be to rely on it. I wanted to deaden my senses as much as possible. How I wished I could hibernate the remainder of winter to wake in spring, healed.

I tried Tylenol PM. Nothing. A girlfriend brought me a care package of lavender bubble bath, soaps, and an eye mask. Supposedly, lavender had sleep inducing properties. It smelled lovely, but it failed to launch me into the deep REM sleep which I so desperately needed.

"I think I should see Dr. Schneiders," I announced to Mark over scrambled eggs, hash browns, crispy bacon, and sour dough toast one morning at IHOP. My appetite had yet to wane. Dr. Schneiders was a neuropsychologist we'd met briefly before surgery; he'd been kind enough to visit me in the hospital. I liked him right away, with his salt-and-pepper beard, compassionate eyes, and soothing voice. His manner was such that you never felt like you belonged in the "crazy" category just because you were seeing a psychologist. He had told me I could call him if I had questions about *anything*. Maybe he could cast a sleep-inducing spell over me I joked to Mark.

He didn't have any spells but did recount a story to us about hypnotizing a patient to sleep. Before I could ask, he said, "No I can't hypnotize you Liz!"

Dr. Schneiders went over behavioral relaxation techniques and explained that part of my problem was I was too impatient trying to reclaim my old life back.

"You had brain surgery," he gently reminded me. "It's going to take weeks and months, maybe longer for you to heal one hundred percent."

But I wanted *all* aspects of my life back. Mark posed the question that was on both our minds:

"Um, doctor, when uh, how long before," he stammered.

"It's normal to want to know about *that!*" Dr. Schneiders half chuckled. "You're not the first to ask."

Sex?

It was my turn to stammer. "But, won't my, I mean..."

Dr. Schneiders assured both of us that it was perfectly safe to make love and, as though reading my mind, added my brain would *not* explode. What a relief *that* was.

I also had other concerns to worry about. Once again, the *What to Expect After Brain Surgery* manual failed to warn me about my body's betrayal.

It was the dead of winter, yet at night my body broke out in drenching sweats as though my internal heater was in overdrive. Was I having panic attacks or hot flashes? Carefully placed washcloths across my forehead proved futile. I slept with the shutters and windows open, peeling off my flannel pajamas and sleeping on top of the comforter. This was insane. Had my pituitary gland's newfound freedom gone straight to its head and skipped pregnancy altogether and instead, propelled me straight into menopause?

Nor could I blame the arid Colorado air for my dry, cracked skin—compliments of my anti-seizure and anti-brain swelling meds. Clumps of my remaining hair were falling out. I felt untouchable and undesirable.

Life moved on while I remained a spectator. The first signs of spring appeared—tiny leaf buds on our Aspen trees, vibrant gold and coral hued tulips emerging from the soil, and the first crop of green blades poking through the dry, wheat colored grass. I spent so much time languishing on the couch that when I left it I half expected to see a permanent imprint of my body on the buttery yellow leather.

It was disheartening to watch Mark take care of the details of my life. The simple act of washing a load of laundry wiped me out for two days. I couldn't concentrate long enough to pay bills or even carry on a conversation. What the hell had been done to my brain? Had it been through an *Extreme Makeover Home Edition* style with rearranged furniture? Brain pushed aside here, there, rewired neurons, and new titanium fittings. Even though I may not like the new décor, I didn't have the luxury of redecorating. I had to live with it for the rest of my life.

Most people like the idea of spending a day curled up in bed, sinking into the latest *New York Times* bestseller or reading the paper cover to cover. I had weeks to engage in my favorite pastime, but even that was beyond me. Words, regardless of their font or color, assaulted my senses. They glared up from their ink stained pages, daring me to absorb them and contemplate their meanings, implied or not. It was all too much.

There were even more brutal attacks. Television characters and news anchors screamed at me in the highest pitch possible. Vivid, quickly moving images jarred my brain. The slightest noise from the hum of the dishwasher to the discordant ring of the telephone was unbearable. The swoosh swoosh of the washing machine was an eerie reminder of the taunting noises I had heard in my head before the tumor was discovered.

And it didn't end there. My body behaved in ways that were completely unnerving. Like the morning I craved a long, luxurious lavender soak in the tub and a clean shave. I'd boost my spirits one-hundred percent with stubble free legs. The airy bubbles covered my flaky skin. Surely, this would help me sleep—if only there was a way to keep the water at eighty-nine degrees, I'd stay in here until I was back on my feet. As I shaved my legs, the bubbles took on a crimson hue. Was this magically changing bubble bath like kids' Crayola markers? Tiny beads of blood had coagulated up and down my calves, knees, and thighs. "Oh, God! I'm going to bleed to death," I screamed, horrified as I reached for a bath towel. White. Big mistake. I was all alone. Mark was out running errands that morning.

I called Dr. Fullagar's office and was instructed to leave a message. When my call was finally returned, I was told that this is "quite normal." Filling your bathtub with blood is normal? Apparently, the anesthesia had compromised my weakened blood vessels. I grabbed a pencil and jotted down another fact also omitted from the *What to Expect After Brain Surgery* manual. Was there anyone else to talk to at this point? What else couldn't I do? I just wanted to feel some semblance of womanhood, femininity. I can't bleed from the right places. I can't sleep. I can't stop eating. My hair is falling out. I can't even shave my legs without dire consequences. I was falling apart and my grip on sanity felt like it was slipping away.

My rant would be better captured in a journal. In an unused

reporter's notebook, I vented away. Maybe revisiting the rudimentary basics of writing—free journaling—would help. I didn't know if any of it would make sense. But it didn't matter. I needed to prove I at least had some control over my own thoughts, and that I could still form some semblance of coherent sentences.

I know I'm scribbling everything I want to remember so this may not be in the best order. I don't want to forget anything.

My biggest challenge is the orders everyone is issuing to me—to relax! I worry about everything. The way I feel and that it's not the way I want to feel. So I'll try an experiment. I'm going to write down everything—get it out in the open and that will be it. Once it's on paper, I can't worry about it any longer.

I hate feeling numb (my greatest discomfort and source of frustration), not sleeping more than a few hours at a stretch, tiring easily, feeling weak, not being able to feel my face, not being able to feel Mark kiss me good morning and good night, feeling good one day and feeling like crap the next, not having the energy to do the things I want—just starting simple tasks, being bald and losing hair, not being able to make plans in advance since I can't gauge how I'll feel on the day I've planned something... Okay, enough ranting already.

Looking at the big picture, I am grateful to be alive and to be here, to have the support of my family, friends, and neighbors, I'm only half numb, I can walk and talk, I can appreciate a sunny day. I survived surgery. I am getting stronger every day. My hair will grow back. I can drive. I can smile, laugh. I will remind myself of these blessings when I am feeling down and alone.

I felt better already and had forgotten how cathartic the journaling experience could be. I promised myself I would journal every day to keep my mind off the unchangeable.

And then the day I'd been dreading arrived—Mark leaving for Florida for spring training. I don't know why, but something finally clicked in me that this must have been even more difficult for him. Not only was he leaving me behind, he had the pressure of pitching well enough to make a team. And we both knew from experience that there were no guarantees.

"We can do this," Mark said after one last hug. "It's not the first time we've been tested in this way."

"I know, I know, hun," I cried.

Within an hour of saying our tearful good-byes, my childhood best friend, Vivian, arrived to take the first shift on the Liz Caretaker/Watchdog Calendar.

"Izza Wizza!" she hollered, when we spotted each other in the airport terminal. It felt great to hear the nickname she'd bestowed upon me many years ago. Viv and I first met in Mr. McKinley's third grade class at Tustin Memorial School in California. She had shiny black hair worn in braids, and sparkling hazel eyes. We became friends over hopscotch. Despite boyfriends, college, different jobs, and changing zip codes, our friendship remained just as strong as our first meeting on that tarmac playground.

"Okay, first things first, Izza Wizza," Viv said. "Let's give your hair a fresh look!"

"Look schmook!" I said. "There's not much to work with here," I said, pointing to my sparse head, courtesy of Craniotomy 101.

Viv gave selflessly of herself for the next ten days. She spoiled me with manicures, pedicures, and nightly massages. She also prepared fabulous gourmet meals—jambalaya, angel hair pasta with shrimp marinara, and chicken fajitas with homemade tortillas.

The most important thing Vivian did for me was to pull me out of the quagmire of self-pity. I could sit around all day and ask *why me?* But I knew as well as Vivian did, it was wasted energy. I just needed to hear it from her.

"Look Liz. I know this is a cliché, but there is a reason for all that you have gone through, and knowing you as well as I do, you will turn it into a positive."

Before Vivian flew home, she left me a letter, which I still keep in my nightstand drawer:

Remember to feed your soul. If only for a few minutes each day, be it through prayer, meditation, music, reading, or finding what to be thankful for each day. You are a wonderful gift and have been given the gift of life so enjoy it. Live each day to its fullest. Breed your creativity—show the world your spirit through the pictures you take and through your writings. Share it with the world. Each day you will grow stronger. Do not look back to the past and live in that fear. That part is over. Carry it with you as something that has helped shape the strong, confident woman you are becoming. See that God has given you life, so cherish it.

On the last day of spring training, I anxiously awaited Mark's call.

"I made the team!" he blurted out before I'd even said hello. He'd be a starting pitcher for the Red Barons, the triple-A affiliate for the Philadelphia Phillies.

"I'm so proud of you," I said.

Just three months after brain surgery, I was on my way to Scranton, Pennsylvania, to reunite with my husband and start living our new life together. The worst was behind me, or so I thought.

CHAPTER FIVE
BEANBALL

I've got a lot of years to live after baseball and I would like to do them with the complete use of my body.—**Sandy Koufax**

Stop worrying about the potholes in the road and celebrate the journey!—**Barbara Hoffman**

A small trouble is like a pebble. Hold it too close to your eye and it fills the whole world and puts everything out of focus. Hold it at a proper distance and it can be examined and properly classified. Throw it at your feet and it can be seen in its true setting, just one more tiny bump on the pathway of life. —**Celia Luce**

Mark, Scranton, and a hotel room two thousand miles away beckoned me. But before Koufax and I could board a plane, I had a critical post-op date with a hollow tube—an MRI.

I returned to the familiar cold hospital hallways with their thick black arrows directing me to neurodiagnostics and radiology. I negotiated the gurney-wide accommodating corridors like a seasoned lab rat in a maze. Before I could have my MRI, the admitting receptionist instructed me to fill out the necessary forms. I'd already had two, what else did they need to know? *Did I have any metal in my body? If so, mark X on the outlined body areas below.* Well, that was easy.

Next question—*did I have any pain or numbness? If so, also mark X on the black outlined body.* There wasn't enough room to indicate my trouble spots. Could I just make a huge X across the entire head? Yes, that would do.

The matronly technician explained what the next forty-five minutes would entail and asked if I was claustrophobic.

"I've had brain surgery," I interjected. "I think I'll be okay."

It took about twenty minutes to complete the preparations necessary before lift off.

Lie flat on back.

Arms at side.

Align head.

Pull straps across forehead to keep head immobile.

Insert IV line.

Fill syringe with gadolinium.

"Okay, we're set," she said. "Just relax and go to sleep if you want," were the last suggestions I heard as I was slowly pulled back, head first, into the tiny space.

As if you could take a much needed cat nap with your brain lit up like the Fourth of July while listening to a cacophony akin to jackhammers on a construction site.

"Are you ready?" the tech's voice boomed through the built-in mic.

"Yes." I was careful not to flinch a muscle or blink an eye, which is no easy feat. Trust me.

"The first set will take eight minutes."

Why is it when you're commanded not to move, your left heel, the small of your back or your right nostril has an itch? To keep myself distracted in the noisy tube, I prayed for a clean MRI. I also prayed that my pituitary gland had returned to its pre-tumor shape, color, and appearance.

When the scans were finally over and I was liberated from the tube, I informed the technician I would personally deliver my films to Dr. Fullagar's office. No more nail biting and floor pacing until the next morning waiting for a verdict. The heavy films—114 images—carried my fate and would foretell my future. I wasn't taking any chances.

While the tech carefully assembled them, I searched her eyes for a sign. Could she interpret the images? If she could, her eyes didn't reveal the answer either way. How many times a day did she neatly assemble a fate she couldn't disclose, unlike fortune tellers with their crystal balls and Tarot cards?

I walked the connecting bridge from the hospital to Dr. Fullagar's office with heavy films in tow. I signed in and took an uncomfortable seat, anxiously awaiting my name to be called. I scanned the faces of other patients. Were they about to be told the same devastating news I'd heard only three months ago? They wore the vacuous expression I knew all too well.

When *Holzemer* was finally called out, I followed a nurse back into one of the meticulously clean examination rooms. I answered the obligatory questions while she checked my vitals. When she left the room, I noticed what looked like my pathology report on the counter.

Was I brave enough to take a sneak peek before Dr. Fullagar walked in? I had to know if my former roommate had complied with its eviction notice or had he left excess baggage behind, such as a frayed toothbrush or a favorite threadbare sweatshirt, as painful reminders of his uninvited stay.

The size and shape of the pituitary gland are normal. There is a focal area of decreased signal noted posteriorly on the enhanced scan. This corresponds to the posterior lobe on the nonenhanced scan and is not felt to represent a space-occupying abnormality.

Whatever all that meant.

Then I scanned further down and read, *"There are no other significant findings."*

"Thank God," I whispered. I was ready to break out into a victory dance in Dr. Fullagar's office with Kool n' the Gang's *Celebration* humming in my head, until a bolded area on the operative report forced me to do a double-take. Even the font was larger. And there were CAPS.

> IMPRESSION: *Surgical cavity (hole) noted in the right middle fossa from resection (removal) of previous meningioma (what, there's more than one?). There may be some residual meningioma lying adjacent to the right cavernous sinus.*

And, as if I needed it spelled out again:

> *A small amount of residual or recurrent tumor cannot be excluded. Continued follow up with attention to these areas is suggested.*

Whoa, whoa—back up! Residual? Recurrent? Suggested? Try these bolded, capped words on for size—FUCKING MANDATORY! I've just read that I may have residual recurrent tumor and a follow up is merely *suggested*? How about if I installed a freestanding MRI machine in my bathroom? I could add it to the list of everyday health maintenance tenets we humans follow—shower, brush teeth, floss, apply deodorant, scan your head, fresh pair of underwear—why not? Think of the millions of dollars health insurance companies would save from preventative health care. No suggestions, just mandates.

I was so transfixed by the report that I didn't notice Dr. Fullagar standing in front of me. Patiently, he went over the report and explained that the findings were quite common and that only one percent of all cases have a problem. He further explained that since I'd only had surgery three months ago, my brain was still shifting back into place, there was excess fluid, and it could be dural thickening as well. What the hell was that? I sure felt like I was thickening because of my appetite, but what was dural? All par for the course Dr. Fullagar reassured me. Another minor fact I wish had been included in the *What to Expect After Brain Surgery* manual. Just forewarn me of the remote possibility that my roommate may return. I also made a mental note that one shouldn't read a path report alone—ever, period.

During the drive home, the words *"Only one percent"* resonated in my head. Even though I had been repeatedly reassured that this was a completely normal, nothing-to-be-concerned-about report, somehow I didn't quite buy that. After all, *I* was the one with the gaping hole in my head and with my luck, I'd apply for and be granted membership in the one percent group. Why not? I hated math and it would be my fortune to become the statistical anomaly. My brilliant mathematician father would love that. Better yet, he could probably create a formula for my chances of having a residual tumor.

Mark called later that night anxious to hear about my follow up appointment.

"Everything's fine," I assured him, not wanting to burden him with my worries. After all, he had enough on his plate trying to make a new team.

"Are you sure, hun?" he asked. "You sound different."

"Tell me about the game you pitched today," I wanted to know, hoping that by quickly changing the subject I was off the hook.

"*Liz,*" he said, not fooled by the tactic.

"I miss you and well, being apart sucks," I confessed. It was true; I just couldn't bring myself to talk about my appointment. Besides, what could Mark do anyway? It was an awful feeling to admit, but crying to him about it wouldn't make him understand the tangible fear I lived and breathed every day.

From our bed, as I recapped the day's events, a dreadful thought took hold. What if my seizures were still lurking, like my recently evicted roommate? I was thankful I hadn't yet experienced any seizures post-op. But how would I know if they were planning an encore performance unless I dared to return to what had often been a pre-surgery seizure trigger—Target? Whether it was the overstimulating rows stacked with merchandise or the brightly lit fluorescent aisles—something about Target had seizure inducing properties. That's it—the next morning, I would willingly tempt a déjà vu to test my theory and allay my fears.

Since waking up long before the sun made its daily debut had become de rigueur of my days, to avoid the morning mayhem I arrived at Target just as it opened.

I grabbed a cart and began my covert mission.

First aisle—home accessories, picture frames. No sharp contrast in colors. So far so good.

Second aisle—tools designed to keep your life organized. Really, could you buy organization? Could these smartly crafted gadgets organize my out-of-control thoughts and obsessions about when I'd return to the old me?

Third aisle—shelves stacked with everything a child required for its first year of existence—taunting me with items I desperately wished I were buying for *my* child.

I continued to peruse up and down each neatly organized aisle. As Target began to buzz with more shoppers, a sense of panic washed over me. I feared seeing them move in fast forward motion like I had experienced before surgery.

"Okay Liz, you can do this," I said to myself.

I ducked behind an aisle of bath products then quickly popped out like a Jack-in-the-box to see if anyone appeared different. No. They looked the same. Best of all, no one had pressed that annoying fast forward button. I was safe. Target—bulls-eye!

I tested my theory a few more times. I probably looked like a complete idiot to those downing Starbucks to cast off their too-early-to-be-shopping-bleary-eyed haze. Maybe they thought they were the ones now having déjà vu seizures. Regardless, I completed my mission with a 100 percent success rate. Thank God. I happily drove home with the next objective in mind—cramming five months worth of clothes into two suitcases and worrying about how Koufax would fare on his first cross country flight.

CHAPTER SIX
SAY IT AIN'T SO

This is like déjà vu all over again.—**Yogi Berra**

Any time you think you have the game conquered the game will turn around and punch you right in the nose.—**Mike Schmidt**

You win a few, you lose a few. Some get rained out. But you got to dress for all of them.—**Satchel Paige**

It was D-Day. My long awaited departure to join Mark.

The glass doors gave way to a familiar scene at any given airport—time consuming, endless lines snaking within the terminal. Even though I was very familiar with Denver International Airport—it *was* the springboard to traveling to Mark's worldwide baseball destinations—I found it intimidating nonetheless. This was my first post-surgery flight and nothing felt familiar.

Koufax had already been tranquilized, checked in, and whisked away by two beefy United agents. All that was left to board was me and my brain with all its metal equipment. But first, I had to conquer the security check, which loomed ahead. *Oh God, please don't let me set off any alarms.*

Then, a horrifying image of me becoming magnetically

attached to the parallel metal bars made my breaths shallow. Would those who were awaiting check-in flee? Or would they form a close-knit circle, curious about the spectacle unfolding in front of them—blonde woman attached at the right side of her head to security bars, awkwardly flapping her arms in desperation. Would they turn around expecting to see Ashton Kutcher yell out, "Surprise, you've been *Punk'd*!"

"Next!" barked an agent, obviously displeased by my hesitation. Setting her off was not on my agenda. I held my breath as I gingerly walked through the security bars. Not a single ear piercing beep greeted me. I'd made it, I silently cheered. A MasterCard ad at its best—

> *Airline ticket to Philadelphia: $377*
> *Canine companion ticket: $250*
> *Not setting off airport alarms: priceless*

I went to my assigned gate. Before boarding, I couldn't help but think of another bizarre scenario. Even though I lived at a higher altitude—5,280 feet—I worried what would happen as the plane made its gradual ascent to ten, then twenty, and eventually thirty-thousand feet? Would I pop a titanium screw or worse, would my bone flap—well, flap?

A petite brunette flight attendant with perfectly pinned back hair greeted me warmly and directed me to seat 7C. I couldn't help myself and blurted out—"Can you check on my dog during the flight and I've had brain surgery and am a little bit, okay, a lot worried, about flying."

"Not a problem about your dog, and you're going to be just fine," she assured me. I settled into my window seat, grateful that the elderly woman next to me was already nose deep in a Mary Higgins Clark thriller. I was so nervous that I didn't want to engage in idle chit chat. I hoped Koufax and I would arrive hassle free. Once airborne, a feeling of giddiness swept over me. I could hardly believe we would see Mark by day's end. All I needed to worry about was safely landing in Philly, ensuring that Koufax and our bags were transferred to the small commuter plane that would take us to Scranton, and running into Mark's arms. Sounded simple enough. After all, I was a brain tumor survivor. I was soaring at 30,000 feet and I was *alive.*

About halfway into the flight, the attendant returned to inform me that Koufax was doing great. What wonderful service I thought, and I wasn't even in First Class.

As we approached our final destination, it felt as if the pilot had offered me a personal panoramic view of the city. The Atlantic sparkled miles below. Commuters made their way across the Walt Whitman and Delaware bridges. It was nearly sunset and the sky had a milky-pink hue. We circled a few times around the Vet, home to the Phillies, where fans spilled in for a three-game home opener. Would I become one of those fans this season, hopeful that this would be the year Mark made his return to the Big Leagues?

An early landing afforded me the luxury of freshening up before I squeezed into the fifteen-seater to Scranton. Was it safe? Where would they stuff Koufax? I hoped he would forgive me for this trip.

Just as I'd managed to get comfortable, the seatbelt light signaled it was already time to descend. A fairly smooth landing and we were there. And just moments later, Mark surrounded me in the protective embrace I missed more than I had realized. His hair was still damp from the after-game shower, and he smelled of Irish Spring soap and Calvin Klein's Eternity.

We said "I love you" to each other and hugged until Koufax whined. He'd been cooped up in his kennel all day.

"Let's get out of here and eat," Mark said. "You must be starving." I couldn't argue with him as the airline food wasn't very substantial.

After dinner, we settled in to the Residence Inn, our temporary home away from home. They were dog-friendly and Mark had already advised the staff about Koufax's arrival. They even kept bowls of dog biscuits and fresh water at the front desk. We were a family again. That night I fell asleep in the crook of Mark's arm and dreamed for the first time since surgery.

It was fortuitous that Mark's team, the Scranton/Wilkes-Barre Red Barons, were on a long home stretch so he wouldn't have to leave anytime soon. We drove to the stadium early the next day so Mark could give me a tour. It was just like old times when we would take a trial run so I wouldn't feel nervous or get lost in our new surroundings.

I returned to the hotel and spent the afternoon playing fetch with Koufax until game time. There was a large grassy area across the hotel from us, which quickly became his new digs. The three of us settled into our baseball summer routine. Mornings were lazily spent at the hotel, exhausting Koufax, and running errands, before I dropped Mark off at the stadium early afternoon. I'd return to the hotel and nap until game time.

I enjoyed watching Mark settle back into his role as a starting pitcher. He'd been a starter for most of his playing career until the last few years when the Angels had him transition to middle relief. He set the tone when his rotation was up every five or so days, as starters do. We both hoped this was the year Mark made his return to the Majors. God knows we could use a lucky hand after the obstacles we'd faced. "Can we ever get a break?" had become our adopted mantra over the years.

In May alone, Mark recorded several wins and a save, not to mention a perfectly executed bunt. Mark had spent most of his playing career with American League teams, and now that he was with a National League organization, he had the chance to bat. It was exciting to watch him hit, especially when he helped his own cause by bringing in another run. Scoreless inning after scoreless inning and nasty curveballs were getting him noticed. One night a Japanese scout watching in the stands approached Mark after the game. He represented the Yokohama BayStars and told Mark they were looking for American players to strengthen their team. "I like what I see," he informed Mark. The idea of living in a foreign country again was exciting but Mark cautioned me not to get my hopes up. After all, the scout *was* only window shopping and I *was* still recovering.

The Red Barons' schedule during May gave Mark and I the opportunity to travel to two cities I'd always dreamed of visiting—Baltimore and Washington, D.C. Mark had been a part of history at Baltimore's famed Camden Yards on September 5, 1995, giving up a home run to Cal Ripken Jr., the night he tied Lou Gehrig's record for most consecutive games ever played.

In Washington, Mark and I spent an emotional day visiting JFK's eternal flame, the endless graves at Arlington National Cemetery, the Tomb of the Unknowns, and the Vietnam Veteran's Memorial. We spent the last few hours at the U.S. Holocaust Memorial Museum. Uncertain of whether I'd ever visit Israel or any European concentration camps, I was curious to know more about my faith and my ancestors. What little I did know were from school textbooks and my paternal grandparents' oral histories on how they had fled Russia and Poland decades before the Nazi invasion.

As we entered the museum, an elderly volunteer handed Mark and me an ID card and booklet with a neatly printed name on the front of each. She explained how each page of the booklet represented a floor of the exhibit, which mirrored the life of the individual we'd been assigned. By the end of our self-guided tour we would learn our fate—would we be a victim of the gas chambers, had we fled to another country, or would we be fortunate enough to escape and live in freedom? Exhibit after exhibit depicted unspeakable atrocities committed against a nation of innocents—their fate sealed by the edicts of the evil dictator, Adolf Hitler. Did they have an inkling of what was to befall them when they were corralled and stripped of everything, including their dignity? At the exhibit's end, Mark learned he had escaped. I had not. Was this an omen of things to come? I was too mentally fatigued by the end of the tour to think of anything else.

We returned to Scranton for another week before flying to Indianapolis for the Memorial Day weekend. I felt guilty leaving Koufax in a kennel again, but supposed it was good to get our "baby" used to the life of a peripatetic baseball family. After all, he was probably the only child we'd ever have.

Not long after we settled into our hotel, Mark received a call from the Japanese scout who'd seen his marvelous performance earlier that month. They were seriously considering him. I couldn't contain my excitement.

"Japan! I've always wanted to live in Asia!" I said, jumping up.

"They're just talking," Mark pointed out. "I'd rather get back to the Majors right now and besides, we just got settled in Scranton."

He was right. My heart said that this was Mark's time. It had to be. He'd lost a job, started over, and watched his wife endure brain surgery all in one year. His time was due.

Twenty-four hours later Mark hit the jackpot when the Red Barons' manager informed Mark that the Phillies had called him up. He was on his way back to "the show." The next day we caught a flight to Philadelphia at an ungodly hour. Mark would wear red jersey #46 and would pitch for the Phillies in Veteran's Stadium—the same stadium I'd flown over less than a month ago.

Upon landing, we raced back to Scranton, rescued Koufax from kennel hell, and returned to Philly to check into yet another hotel with just enough time for Mark to make it to practice. I collapsed on the hotel bed and surprisingly, woke in time to get ready for the game.

As I drove into the players' parking lot filled with the latest luxury cars and SUVs, I felt a wet sensation across my forehead. Nervousness? No. Humidity? No. Philly was known for that in the summer, but it was only early June. I wiped my brow only to feel more dampness. I looked into the rearview mirror and gasped. A small pool of liquid had formed adjacent to my part line where my incision had been. I carefully dabbed at it with a handful of Kleenex and hurried to Will Call for my ticket. The Phillies were hosting a 3-game home opener against the Red Sox. It was interleague play at its best and I wasn't going to let a little fluid spoil my night. Not this one.

I settled into my seat and absorbed the sights and sounds of baseball on a perfect June night. I relished the medley of accents—"*Yo, Yo*" from Joysey; "*It's outta here*" from Philly; and "*Where'd ya pawk ya cawr*" from Boston. A melting pot symphony. Beautiful. And it was even more perfect as I watched Mark make his Phillies major league debut. He faced one lefty and struck him out. He was back.

So caught up in the excitement as a proud baseball wife, I'd forgotten all about the scary moment I'd experienced earlier, until Mark and I returned to the hotel after celebrating his first victorious outing. I immediately went into the bathroom to check on my leaking head, and gasped when once again I saw fluid dripping from my incision. In the harsh light I could now see it was the color of chicken broth and elastic in consistency, like rubber cement.

"My brain is leaking," I said to Mark, scared. "This doesn't seem right!"

I mopped the leak with a washcloth but even light pressure caused it to ooze more.

"Just leave it alone, you'll make it worse," Mark warned me. "You're still healing."

I hoped he was right as I tossed and turned all night wondering if this was normal. I had nothing to compare it to. I'd never had brain surgery before, so how was I to know? Did I need to fly home? What if my brain oozed out next? As if I needed to lose more brain cells. Maybe I could invent an oozing-gray-matter plug similar to a wine cork.

The next morning, the oozing had stopped. Even so, I wasn't taking any chances. I called Dr. Fullagar's office and was politely informed he was vacationing out of the country with his family. The receptionist took our number and said she'd have someone call me back.

Not wanting to waste any time, Mark called the Phillies' main office for the name of a local neurosurgeon. When I dropped Mark off at the stadium, the Phillies' director of baseball met us in the parking lot and said she'd already set up an appointment for me at the University of Pennsylvania. I'd forgotten all about the Big League baseball perks: better seats, private parking lot, and quicker access to doctors.

"Being in the Big Leagues doesn't mean anything to me if you're not healthy," Mark assured me when we arrived at 3400 Spruce Street the next morning.

Dr. Eric Zager saw me promptly. Like Dr. Fullagar, he didn't look much older than forty. Fortunately, I always traveled with my bulging-at-the-seams medical file, which he'd had time to review earlier.

No sooner had he examined my oozing orifice, than he said the unthinkable.

"I want you to check into the hospital for surgery—now."

"What?"

"There's a chance you have a CSF (cerebrospinal fluid) leak and we can't take any chances," he continued. Meningitis was mentioned and a host of other multi-syllabic words. I was still translating the foreign language I had painfully mastered not so long ago, while Dr. Zager continued.

"I'll operate first thing tomorrow morning." The words hung over my head like an ominous cloud. No. No. Not again.

I looked to Mark to tell me this wasn't real. He was stunned. Who the hell had pressed the rewind button? This wasn't supposed to happen; I was only supposed to see the doctor as a precautionary measure. As Monty Python once said, *It's nothing—just a flesh wound.* Right?

Within moments, Dr. Zager's office assistant came over with a sheaf of papers for me to sign and explained I'd be assigned a room within the hour. My world had spun out of control. I shoved the papers away and felt a wave of tears streaming down my cheeks.

"All I want is to have a baby," I shrieked, the sobs becoming heavier. I couldn't move. I didn't want to. Within twelve hours, I'd be back on the front lines defending my life. It was time to face the grim reality that my body might never be capable of creating a son or daughter of my own.

Mark gently took my arm and led me to the hospital at U-Penn, where I was checked in. It was déjà vu all over again, only this time, I had my own well-appointed room. I thought if I tried hard enough, I could actually convince myself I was checking in to a nice resort and could go downstairs later to enjoy happy hour cocktails by the pool. Freshly polished cherry wood furniture, nicely made up bed, plush carpet. I searched for the stack of travel guides—"*How to Pass the Time Before Your Second F!@*ing Craniotomy!*" and "*Top 10 Things to Experience in Your Life Before You Die and Brain Surgery Isn't One of Them!*"—but couldn't find them.

I felt like I was in prison, except I hadn't been allowed to make my one phone call. Should I worry my parents? Call my best friend?

I couldn't bring myself to do either. How could this be happening?

"I can't do this again," I cried.

"Yes you can," Mark reassured me. "You're strong and you've done it before."

"But I don't want to," I cried harder.

It had been nearly four months since my first surgery. I was well on my way to recovery, or so I had thought. All but one medication had been eliminated from my life. My hair was finally growing in and now I'd have to revisit my post-op Mohawk.

Even though I was told this surgery would be less invasive because the bone flap wouldn't have to be removed, I wondered how I would survive.

In the early morning of June 7, 2000, I had my second craniotomy.

Three hours later, I came to and once again was asked if I could count the number of fingers being held up in front of me. Despite my anesthesia-induced haze, I understood the good news that Dr. Zager had successfully drained an excess pocket of CSF, which should clear everything up. I'd survived my second brain surgery in four months. Surely now I'd truly be on the road to recovery. The bad news was that Mark had to leave for a road trip to Baltimore less than twenty-four hours later.

How could I go back to the hotel alone? I doubted Marriott maids were trained to look after guests recovering from their second craniotomy.

"Hi, this is Room 222. Could you please send up fresh towels, gauze, and cotton balls? I have a head wound to plug up."

I never checked back into our hotel. Fortunately, a lovely family of one of Mark's teammates was gracious enough to take Koufax and me under their wing. I slept most of the weekend and marveled at the unexpected turn my journey had taken.

When Mark returned from his Orioles road trip, we settled into an apartment and back into our routine, except there's nothing routine about starting all over again. I battled against loneliness and coming to grips with all that I'd been through. I just wanted to hold on to some semblance of the former Liz—the funny, easy going, spontaneous soul who had already accomplished so much in her short span of thirty-two years—

taking a *Thelma & Louise* adventure—sans Thelma—against my father's wishes in my trusty, 150,000+ miles Honda Accord that had been packed with what little I had accumulated in life because I wanted to experience everything for the first time alone when I arrived at my new life in Boulder to start graduate school; meeting my future husband one weekend knowing, as we sat in front of a Vancouver rose garden in Queen Elizabeth Park after a minor league ball game, that *he* was the one; forgoing a lavish wedding on New Year's Eve and eloping to Sin City in front of a French minister just seven months after I had made Mark ask me twice, on bended knee in the Steamboat Springs' snow, to marry him; riding rusty buses throughout Venezuelan palm tree lined streets, and snapping black and white photographs of eager children, who were curious about my fair skin and pale eyes. I was no longer that Liz.

Sleep was futile even with Koufax's reassuring presence throughout the quiet, humid nights. During Mark's next road trip, I called Amber and my tears welled up even before she'd said hello.

"Why do I spend an hour in the shower every morning because it takes me that long to wash away the tears and that's all I have the energy to do?" I asked. And, "What kind of supportive wife am I when I'm too exhausted by seven p.m. to drive to the stadium, and instead I have to watch my husband record another strike out on our rented television?" I sobbed.

Amber allowed me to vent away without interruption. Teaching kindergartners for years had honed her skills as a patient listener. As always, she knew how to comfort me.

"Liz, you're expecting too much too soon," she said. "I know it's cliché, but God has a plan for you."

I wanted to believe her, but I had my doubts. What is the meaning behind having your brain probed and your upstairs furniture rearranged all over again?

I don't remember how long I rambled on, but when I hung up, I knew what I had to do—throw myself a pity party. I should have done it after my first surgery and purged it out of my system once and for all. It would be a blowout and I couldn't wait.

Instead of setting out the best china and freshly polished silverware I didn't own, I lined the table with boxes of Kleenex, tubs of Ben & Jerry's chocolate chip cookie dough ice cream, pizza, and my favorite CDs—Gloria Gaynor's *I Will Survive* and Lesley Gore's *It's My Party*. What an exhilarating feeling to shout, dance, and at the same time, curse at what my tumor had done to me—zapped my energy, alienated me, created doubt in my writing abilities, affected my relationships with loved ones, robbed me of children, caused me 24/7 pain. It had invaded my life, not once, but twice. But no more.

I will survive was fucking right. A few weeks later with Mark on yet another road trip, I set out on a new mission—to prove to myself that nothing, not even two brain surgeries, would prevent me from living my life. I packed up our truck and Koufax and I traveled to Long Island, New York, to visit with a friend I hadn't seen in years.

White knuckled driving over the Outerbridge Crossing and Verrazano-Narrows bridges in lunch hour traffic and navigating en route to Long Island further proved that I could survive anything.

Spending the weekend sleeping in and reconnecting with Bonnie, her husband, John, and daughter, Holly, was better than anything my doctors could have prescribed. Bonnie and I had met years ago when Mark and John were California Angel teammates. She had faced infertility too and was always so encouraging about my having a baby. Now she was mom to miracle Holly—I relished watching the two of them interacting. Holly's impromptu hugs and "I love you's" melted me. I would never forget Bonnie's parting words that weekend, "It will happen for you too when the time is right." Her words resonated while Koufax and I made the drive back to Philly. I mentally recorded another victory for myself.

I was making baby steps.

CHAPTER SEVEN
HIT FOR THE CYCLE

It could be, it might be, it is! A home run!—**Harry Caray**

I am woman! I am invincible! I am pooped!—**Author Unknown**

I would like it if men had to partake in the same hormonal cycles to which we're subjected monthly. Maybe that's why men declare war—because they have a need to bleed on a regular basis.—**Brett Butler**

We were home. Koufax and I readjusted to post-surgery life back in our own house again.

Mark's season ended in mid-September after the Red Barons were eliminated in the first play-off round. By the end of the month, my follow up appointment with the neurologist delivered great news—I could spend the next several weeks weaning myself off the anti-seizure medication, Neurontin. I was seizure free and soon to be medication free. No more twice daily pills to remember.

As I gradually reduced my dosage, I became increasingly tired. This seemed odd, since I had always believed the meds *were* the cause of much of the malaise and sluggishness I had felt ever since surgery. I told myself again that my body had undergone tumultuous changes over the last seven months. It's just part of the brain tumor journey, although it was more like a *Survivor* island nightmare. Where would my journey take me next?

I soon found out the next morning—bent over the toilet, my belly knotted like a clenched fist. Please don't let me die, I pleaded to no one in particular. Koufax bounded up the stairs and pressed his refreshingly cool nose against my face. A SNAG—A Sensitive New Age Guy with maternal instincts. I gripped the porcelain bracing myself for the worst. Nothing. The feeling had passed as suddenly as it had taken hold. But when I stood up, a gushing sensation emanated from deep within my loins.

"Oh my God," I shrieked, as a brilliant red river of blood streamed down my inner thighs. My Victoria's Secret floral cotton shorts quickly saturated. I couldn't mop up the blood quickly enough. I soon ran out of towels.

"Oh God," I cried again, but it wasn't in horror this time. It finally registered—the drought had ended and I was having a period. My first in eighteen long months. Tears of elation and joy literally poured out of me.

This time I *could* break out into a celebratory dance! I scrambled for the phone to call Amber, not worried about leaving a trail of blood behind me. After all, I didn't have any Kotex—they had long been thrown out, about the same time I'd flushed my last packet of birth control pills down the toilet.

"Amber, Amber," I shrieked into the receiver when she picked up.

"What's wrong," she asked groggily.

"I'm bleeding!" I gasped as another sharp cramp hit me. "Hear me roar," I shouted. "I am woman again!"

CHAPTER EIGHT
SCREWBALL

It was a cross between a screwball and a changeup. It was a screw-up.—**Bob Patterson**

Success is not measured by what you accomplish, but by the opposition you have encountered, and the courage with which you have maintained the struggle against overwhelming odds.—**Orison Sweet Marden**

You spend a good piece of your life gripping a baseball and in the end it turns out that it was the other way around all the time.—**Jim Bouton**

"But doctor," I pleaded, during an appointment with my fertility specialist, "are you saying I may not be ovulating even though I've had my first period in eighteen months?"

My heart sank. My roommate had been evicted. I was med free. I was bleeding. Yet he was telling me matter-of-factly that I still might not become pregnant. I wished I'd known this back in high school. How many times had I heard Miss Thurston lecture about how easy it was to become pregnant inadvertently?

"You're the case study we read about in medical school, but

never come across in practice," he said, trying to console me.

Thanks Doc, I thought to myself, but it was of little comfort. Again, our mantra, *"Can we ever get a break?"* repeated in my head.

So here I was—case study in the flesh! What could I do?

He said if Mark and I wanted to expand our family, our best chance—save for adoption—was in-vitro. I'd have to take daily hormonal injections. The thought of needles sent my head spinning. I know, I know! I've had drills, blades, and saws tear through my cranium, not once, but twice, yet I was feeling squeamish over needles?

"Where," I barely breathed, "do I inject myself? In my stomach, like a diabetic?"

"No, in your back side," he said, grinning. "Mark can practice on an orange; most of my clients do this a few times to become comfortable with the process."

It registered—I would be subjected to daily injections in my ass and I'd have to put my trust in Mark. Now this was getting complicated. What a cruel way to conceive a child, I thought.

In the meantime, he sent me home with a graph note pad and instructions on how to chart my basal temperature first thing each morning. Perhaps we could determine an ovulatory pattern.

Once again I'd been reduced to statistical anomalies—at twenty-nine, I was a decade too old to have the particular kind of breast tumor I'd had; at thirty-two, I was two decades too young to have a meningioma brain tumor; four months after my first craniotomy, I fell into the statistical unlikelihood of being in the one percent category of patients who had complications from brain surgery; and the final insult—at thirty-three, it appeared as though my ovaries had cashed in their chips.

I grabbed my graphs and headed to Walgreens for a thermometer. Being a woman with defective parts was wonderful.

As the days grew short and dark with the onset of autumn, mine began with me neatly penciling in my temperature on the graphs. Soon, the charts took on the appearance of narrow mountain peaks, representing the narrow window of opportunity I had each month to become pregnant. And I prayed every month that this would be the one when my body *wouldn't* defy me.

When carved pumpkins and scarecrows adorned porches in our neighborhood, I felt the familiar onset of moodiness and cramps.

"I have a theory," I smiled to Mark over breakfast one day.

"Huh, Hun?" he mumbled, momentarily lifting his gaze from the sports page.

"I believe," I continued, slightly irritated that the World Series box scores merited greater attention than my lower extremities, "my pituitary is free to breathe again and fully alive now that the pressure of my tumor is no longer there!" I said excitedly. "We can have a baby now!"

"I think the doctors know what they're talking about," Mark said, returning his gaze to the paper. "Let's just go ahead with our plan to start in-vitro after the holidays."

Maybe Mark was right. We had Major League health insurance, it was the off-season, and there was no sense worrying about what I couldn't control. I'd sure learned *that* lesson painfully enough this year.

I also couldn't control the ever-increasing tension I felt along my double incision and the right side of my face. It felt like it was being pulled in opposite directions, like salt water taffy being made in candy store fronts. As a child, I had watched in wonderment as skilled workers stretched the multi-colored candy to amazing lengths. Pulled to the point of extreme without breaking, yet maintaining its consistency. I hoped my face would exhibit the same resiliency. I'd been told that during my second surgery, Dr. Zager had to pull back facial muscle to prevent another CSF leak. I knew I'd always been thin-skinned and now I had the proof in my path report.

Then, one afternoon while running errands, I couldn't help but notice an alarming sight in my car mirror as I changed lanes. The upper right corner of my lip was curling upward. *Oh my God*, I screamed, nearly rear-ending the car in front of me. I dared to look in the mirror again—I had a quivering lip. Had my body been possessed by Elvis? To make matters worse, my lip had a rhythmic pulsating beat too. Would I break into a rendition of *Hound Dog* next?

Days later, I met with my neurologist, who suggested a Botox treatment.

"But I thought that was only for wrinkles?"

My neurologist launched into the merits of Botox and how it could also dull the excruciating pain I lived with day to day.

As she further explained its paralyzing properties, it made sense. If you could unfurrow a brow, why not uncurl a snarl?

I could be treated on the spot.

How fortuitous I didn't have time to consider the fact I was about to have poison injected into my face. While she extracted live botulism from a vial, I braced myself in the name of vanity.

"I'll start with the right side first," she explained, as I gripped the leather armrests.

Nothing. Just the sensation of pressure. It was surprisingly painless. Then again I *was* numb along the right side of my face.

"Okay, now the left," she continued. "This is to balance your face."

This made sense, as the last thing I wanted to do was bill my insurance for a lopsided visage.

I relaxed, figuring it was smooth sailing so far.

"Holy crap!" I shouted from pain. I was afraid to breathe in case I was accidentally injected with too much Botox. Society ladies willingly paid for this? Just for vanity's sake?

Several painful pinpricks later, I had undergone my first cosmetic procedure in the name of Elvis.

I returned home already feeling years younger. Now this was the upside to having a brain tumor.

Another upside to having a brain tumor was my new founded talent of predicting the weather. My face had become a weather vane and got tightened when clouds and inclement conditions were on the horizon. Rain, thundershowers, and a sudden cold front—the right side of my face predicted it all. I decided against contacting my local TV stations and sharing my secrets—after all, they had spent millions on their Doppler Radar and Accu-Forecasts technology, not to mention padded paychecks for their on-air talent. It didn't take long before Mark began checking in with me from work—"Liz, can you tell me if I can get 18 in today or should I just shoot for nine?"

My body delivered again with cramps and another period. I couldn't hide my glee from the Safeway clerk when I purchased another box of Super, Super Absorbency Kotex and a bottle of Advil to dull the killer cramps.

I was bleeding again, had a balanced face—life was looking up.

Until I retrieved yet *another* baby announcement from my community's standard-issue metal mailbox.

"Mmmm, let's see who is child productive today," I mused, tearing open the envelope.

Twins. Great. A double slap in the ovary.

I lived in the fastest-growing-master-planned-family-oriented suburban county in the entire United States and I couldn't even contribute to the population explosion. Not only was I incapable of carrying life in my womb, but I was regularly tormented by baby shower invitations and birth announcements.

Maybe it was time for me to send out my own announcement. After all, I had given birth, in a sense. The labor was excruciating and I had the permanent scars to prove it. A ten-year gestation period was nothing to be ashamed about. Yes, that was it! I beamed like a proud mother as I rushed back into the house for art supplies, and let my creative juices take over.

A few hours later, I was still beaming, pleased with my accomplishments. I might not be a mother, but I could put on a "proud" mother face for a child who had created the perfect masterpiece.

After ten years in the making...
Mark and Liz are proud to announce the birth of
Enormous right middle third sphenoid wing meningioma
February 11, 2000
54.04 mm
Weight uncertain but one heavy fucker, that's for sure

I made copies and addressed envelopes, furiously. Oh to be a fly on the wall to observe my family's and friends' reactions would be priceless. Childless? Yes. Humorless? No.

Over the next few weeks, I became an expert at charting my ovulatory patterns. Then, the day after Christmas, I had my annual ob-gyn visit. She went over the last few "interesting"— as she put it—months of my life. Just like my fertility doctor, she said it was a good sign my body was getting back on track again, but also wanted to take blood samples to check my hormone levels.

Later that day she called. My heart sank when I recognized her voice. In my experience, it was a bad omen when doctors called you at home.

"Liz, are you sitting down?" she asked. "I have some news for you."

CHAPTER NINE
KNOCK THE COVER OFF THE BALL

Don't look back. Something might be gaining on you.
—Satchel Paige

If the dream is big enough, the facts don't count.**—Dexter Yeger**

The moment a child is born, the mother is also born. She never existed before. The woman existed, but the mother, never. A mother is something absolutely new.
—Bhagwan Shree Rajneesh

Oh God, I thought. The air grew thick. *No!* I don't want to hear any news, especially not from a doctor, thank you.

"Congratulations. You're pregnant!"

I lost my balance and nearly toppled over the kitchen bar stool.

"You're pregnant!" the voice repeated, in case I hadn't heard it the first time. I'd certainly heard her, but it *had* to be a mistake.

"Wh-what, are you sure?" I stuttered, thinking that surely she'd called the wrong patient. But, this is impossible. I don't have viable eggs, I wanted to shout back.

"Blood work is pretty accurate," she reassured me. "You're six weeks along."

I was congratulated once more and instructed to call her

office on Monday to schedule my first pre-natal visit.

I held the receiver in my shaking hand for God knows how long, unsure of whether to cry, scream, or shout first. I had a human life inside me that was *already* six weeks old? How did this happen? Well, I knew the rudimentary basics of course, but what about in-vitro and doctors' skepticism and... A host of thoughts and emotions swirled in my head.

I was going to be a mom! I carefully placed my hands on my belly and uttered my first words to my unborn child.

"I love you."

Did I look any different? I began to run upstairs, but then walked—after all I had another life to be responsible for—and tore off my clothes. Maybe it was too soon but my belly didn't look any different. It still didn't seem possible that I had a child growing inside of me.

I had to tell Mark, but he wasn't home. I couldn't just call him with this monumental, earth shattering, ground breaking, not-supposed-to-happen-for-us, miraculous news. And it would be even worse leaving him a voice message:

> *Hi hun, guess what? I have viable eggs after all. In fact, remember how we had a little bit too much to drink at that nice restaurant back in November? Well, your future son or daughter is already six-weeks-old. By the way, could you stop by the store on the way home? I forgot a few things. Thanks, love you.*

No, that wouldn't do either.

I'd always dreamed of how I would tell Mark—I'd set an extra place setting at the dinner table hoping he'd fall for the bait and ask who was joining us. Then I'd coyly smile and say, "You'll find out in nine months!"

I knew what I had to do. I grabbed a stack of magazines out of our recycling bin and started clipping letters. Not of the Ted Kaczynski-Unabomber-threat-letter sort. Within no time I had fashioned what I thought was a clever way of disclosing Mark's impending fatherhood. After all, I'd only have *one* chance to tell him he'd be a father for the *first* time.

When Mark finally arrived home, he immediately suspected something was going on.

"What's up?" he asked, shifting his head to see what I was holding behind my back.

"This is for you," I offered, hoping he wouldn't notice the tears already welling up.

"Is it a fan letter?" he asked, still holding it, rather than ripping it open like I hoped he would.

"No! Just open it!" I couldn't stand the suspense any longer.

I studied Mark's face carefully, wanting to forever imprint on my mind his expression upon first discovering we had created a child. No test tubes. No hormonal injections. Syringe free. Nor did we have to bankroll our home to pay for an invasive procedure.

He was speechless.

His brows knotted up in his signature style when something sounded too good to be true.

I can't wait to meet you, Daddy, he read out loud once. Then a second and third time, still trying to make sense of the colorful array of letters, neatly pasted on a piece of construction paper that was now shaking.

"You mean, you, us...?" his voice trailed off.

"Yes, yes," I cried, and we embraced.

I would explain the details of my doctor's call later, but for now, all that mattered was relishing the knowledge that we were going to be mother-father, mom-dad, ma ma, da da.

The days flew by as we relayed the news to family and friends, ushering in the New Year with a cautious sip of champagne, eagerly absorbing every word of the pregnancy bible—*What to Expect When You're Expecting*. A girlfriend, twice blessed with kids, had given it to me when she heard the news we'd soon be joining the ranks of sleep-deprived parents. I bubbled with emotion and to make it even sweeter, we'd be spending our pregnancy together against the beautiful backdrop of Yokohama, Japan. Just before Christmas, the interested scout who'd seen Mark in Scranton had called and made an offer—one we couldn't refuse. A one-year contract to pitch for the Yokohama BayStars. It was all happening so fast—baseball, baby on the way...

Mark left in mid-January for spring training in Okinawa—it would be a grueling six weeks for him. But unlike previous trips, our goodbyes wouldn't be as difficult—we were now making sacrifices for our baby. The day before he left, I had my first of many pre-natal appointments.

Mark and I were told our baby's expected due date was September 5-10, 2001. A week long due date? God, I hoped I wouldn't be in labor that long. Before we left, my doctor offered something totally unexpected to both of us.

"Would you like to hear the baby's heartbeat?" she asked.

"You can hear it this early?" Mark asked, surprised.

While she spread cool jelly across my still-not-pregnant-looking belly, Mark held my hand. "Hmmm," the doctor mused. "Sometimes it's hard to pick up." No sooner had she spoken than a faint thumping became audible. It grew stronger.

Tears gushed. Smiles broadened. It was *real* now—our baby had a heartbeat and it was strong and fast.

I spent the next six weeks packing and spoiling Koufax as much as possible. He'd have a relative stay with him and look after the house, but it would still be difficult to leave behind the loyal companion who had helped and seen me through my surgeries and recoveries.

Then the date of my first anniversary of what I dubbed my "second chance" at life arrived—February 11, 2001. A tumultuous year had passed and in that time I'd survived two craniotomies, suffered mental anguish over the fact that artificial means were probably my only hope of procreating and finally, in a complete turnaround, my body had defiantly proven doctors wrong. To top it off, I would soon be living in the second largest city in Japan.

Before I began my new journey, I had some unfinished business to attend to—it was time to unlock the mysteries of my bulging-at-the-seams path report, which had tormented me for months. It held secrets I hadn't been prepared to unearth. How did doctors excavate my tumor? Why did it take half a day? I figured if I was going to be a proper mother that I'd better get used to gory details.

I quickly thumbed through the multi-colored tabs—Yellow: Radiology; Red: Pathology; Pink: Insurance; Orange...until I stopped at Aqua: Hospital. Nine pages of Arial, nine point font revealed the secrets to *Meningioma Master Plan Eviction*.

The first two pages were straightforward—how I was positioned on the operating table and then shaved. Next, the foreign language and horror show began, which more than made up for the previous easy-to-digest introduction. I learned that my temporal bone was thin. In fact, it was *almost paper thin, and very easily was cracked, drilled through and bent.* My cranium was literally cracked open, as I had long suspected. Why not just place my head in an oversized nutcracker and gently squeeze until shattered?

Bipolar electrocautery was utilized as well as a large Leksell, Midas Rex, a 15 blade and for a lovely touch—a corkscrew to pop open my dura. I continued to scan down until I came across this heart stopping description—*The CUSA (Cavitron Ultra-sonic Aspirator) was used to try to debulk the tumor but the tumor was so tough and fibrous that it would not adequately work. Using an attachment, a ring attachment on the Bovie, this was used to internally decompress the tumor.*

I had an image of the trademark mustard yellow Stanley Steemer cleaner vans delivering super powered vacuums to suck out my stubborn roommate. Did I really want to continue on? I'd made it this far; there was no point turning back now.

And then..."*At this point, utilizing the bipolar electrocautery, the biopsy forceps, several various-sized patties were taken of tumor.*"

I couldn't help but think of McDonald's.

Meningioma Melt and super-size the fries please.

This tumor was hard, fibrous, the operative report made particular mention of a second time. Well, what did they expect—it had been adhered to my brain for the last ten years. Why would it want to leave all the comforts of home—free room and board and a plentiful food source?

I had narrowly escaped having a blood transfusion, and my bone flap was secured in place with three bone buttons. While that explained the three indentations I could feel in my head, similar to a bowling ball, it also raised more questions. Whose bone was now residing in my head—I certainly wasn't missing any of mine that I was aware of—and what if a button gradually unthreaded itself? I wasn't much of a seamstress, but I didn't like the thought of loose bone buttons floating around in a pool of cerebrospinal fluid.

I'd had enough. Next mission—spend the remainder of the day alone in quiet reflection and focus on the gift of life growing inside of me, and for once, celebrate me. What better way to do that than to indulge in an escape I'd never taken before—yes, an entire day at the local spa was what the doctor ordered! My body had endured assault after assault the past year; it was time to be nurtured. A day of pampering—facial, pre-natal massage, manicure, and pedicure—would be perfect. I'd already read in my pregnancy bible how important it was for the mother-to-be to embrace her pregnancy and indulge herself. What's good for mommy must be good for baby, right?

A few days later, I received a special Valentine's gift when the first snapshot of my baby was taken during my second pre-natal check up. Because of my high risk history, I was entitled to more ultrasounds than normal—my baby would already have a full photo album before the delivery. I was transfixed by the miniaturized version detailed in black and white. I could actually make out its face—eyes, nose, lips, all there—and its tiny hands and feet tucked under its chin, held close to its chest as if trying to keep warm. Creating life was truly a miracle—one I thought I'd never be capable of experiencing for myself.

"How big is the baby?" I wanted to know.

"Three centimeters," the doctor said. "That's about an inch long and weighing less than an ounce."

Now it was *truly* real. Not only had I heard proof of my baby's existence, I had visual evidence as well. I hurried home with the first stack of snapshots of my child, anxious to send them to Mark. Even though he was deep in REM sleep in an Okinawa hotel room, I quickly scribbled a note and faxed the following Valentine's gift overseas...

Dear Mark, Happy Valentine's Day! I hope you can see this. I'm officially ten weeks and three days. She is already an inch long. xoxo, Liz

She? What had made me write that? Somewhere buried deep in my subconscious did I know? Growing up with three brothers, I always cherished the one-on-one time I had with my mother when she took me out for "girl's day" to watch artsy films at the equally artsy theatre by the beach or when she spoiled me with decadent Swenson's sundaes after a track meet. It would be months before I would know. Despite being polled by family and friends wondering if I'd wait until the birth, my standard response every time was the same.

"I've had enough unknown masses growing inside of me; I'm going to find out what this one is as soon as I can."

But first, I had a date with a sixteen-hour flight to reunite once again with Mark.

The BayStars spoiled the baby and me with a first class seat. Now *this* was the way to travel. The flight began with green tea being served and a generous meal of traditional Japanese cuisine. I was already in love with Japan before I'd even set foot on its soil.

I arrived at Narita International Airport at 4:03 p.m., exactly as my itinerary had stated. My, the Japanese are precise. Surprisingly, I was newly energized just in time to meet Mark at Customs.

"You're starting to show," Mark said happily. It was finally real for him now too.

"I know," I smiled, elated with my burgeoning belly.

As is customary in baseball life, I spent the next few weeks becoming familiar with my new surroundings. We had an apartment overlooking Yokohama Bay—former home to WWII expatriates. I had arrived during one of the loveliest times of the year, cherry blossom season. Tiny pink buds opening for the first time made for an amazing and breathtaking spectacle. I was awed by this new culture and wanted to take everything in. My mornings were spent snapping slices of life pictures of school children and talented Japanese artists sketching in the nearby park; befriending neighbors who allowed me to take their labs, Bris, and Lons on walks so I wouldn't feel Koufax-sick; and admiring the elderly as they pedaled to the nearby open air markets. During the afternoons, the baby and I had a standing date with the couch for a needed nap—until game time arrived and I joined the throngs of excited and loyal fans as they cheered for their BayStars.

Not only did Mark's schedule afford him Mondays off after early morning practice, but it gave us the chance to spend quality time together unlike any previous baseball season. It was as if our mantra, *"Can we ever get a break?"* had finally been heard and answered, and God was being more than generous. I hadn't experienced a day of morning sickness. I lit up rainy days with my twenty-four hour pregnancy glow. We were thankful for the small things—eating dinners together, hand in hand walks to the train station, and visiting the great Buddha, where Mark had snapped a picture of my belly in comparison to the ancient sculpture's. The icing on the cake was landing a freelance assignment with my local paper back home. I'd agonized over whether or not I could revitalize my writing career since surgery, especially with the difficulty I had with spelling, determining the right verb usage, and adhering to AP Style. The sports editor was sold on the query letter I'd sent months earlier to write about baseball in Japan from an American wife's point of view. I wasn't a brain damaged article after all! Baseball had fallen into place, a baby, and now a byline.

Mark's team had arranged for me to see Dr. Suzuki, an ob-gyn not far from our apartment. The team's interpreter, Yas, accompanied Mark and me during each appointment.

"I've been with you to more appointments than I did when my wife had our two kids," he said.

In early June, when Japan's rainy season was in full swing, I went for a 3-D color ultrasound. Mark and I spent an anxious hour at the hospital waiting for an available tech. Wow, first a black and white and now a color photo for my collection. The technician was very thorough and explained everything for Yas, who in turn translated for Mark and me. All the baby's vital structures and organs appeared normal. And then a blank look registered across Yas' face.

"What's wrong?" I asked, with growing concern.

"The technician is asking if you would like to know the sex of the baby," Yas replied.

"Yes!" Mark and I said in unison.

"He says you're having a girl."

A daughter.

My self-prophecy had come to fruition.

Our Hannah Elizabeth—the name we had already chosen. "Hannah in Japanese is *Ha Hana Ko*," Yas said, "which means *flower blossom*."

And as if almost on cue, Hannah announced her presence with a firm kick as though to say, "I'm here, Mom."

I didn't think I would truly believe it until I actually held her in my arms for the first time. I spent the remainder of the day floating—so this is what it meant to be high.

In light of my history, it was our decision whether to have Hannah in Japan or in Colorado. The BayStars season wouldn't wrap up until early October, not including the playoffs—if they made it that far—and I learned that players weren't usually allowed time off to be present at their wives' labor. Also, we had been warned of some complications that could arise during the birth and, coupled with the shocking fact epidurals were not usually prescribed in Japan, I decided that enduring another separation from Mark was the best course of action for Hannah and me.

Mark and I spent the last few weeks of my time in Japan enjoying our final days as just a couple. The day before my flight we traveled to Mt. Fuji on the bullet train. I was taken aback by its snowcapped peaks and grandeur. I appreciated all that it represented. Even though I was unable to physically climb it, in my mind, I had scaled Mt. Fuji in the past year.

I returned home and was literally showered with baby showers. Hannah still had two months before her entry into the world yet she already had a first year wardrobe, every imaginable gadget and toy, and a floral-themed nursery I lovingly decorated for her with Japanese souvenirs. I took Lamaze and breastfeeding classes and anxiously awaited word from Mark when he'd be allowed to fly home, praying it would be before Hannah's arrival.

Labor. I hadn't given it much thought before and preferred NOT to focus on all the gory horror stories girlfriends had shared. How hard could it be? I'd had two brain surgeries, mind them. Then again, what might transpire during labor? What if I pushed too hard and a screw, or one of those bone buttons, came undone? I could imagine the ping ping of a titanium screw or plate reverberating in the labor and delivery room. Now that would be a story—I could already see the headlines:

"Brain Tumor Survivor Pops Out Screws and Baby During Labor."

"It's Titanium Twins!"

But all my worrying was for naught. Mark arrived just in time for us to enjoy a few more days on our own before life changed forever. Despite not knowing what to expect or how it would feel, I awoke days later with a pain I knew must have signaled labor. Maybe it had been the extra spicy salsa the night before. Mark quickly made the fifteen minute drive to the hospital, ensuring I didn't miss the opportunity for an epidural. Eleven exhausting hours later, and with one last great push on the count of ten, a healthy Hannah Elizabeth Holzemer made her long anticipated entrance into the world, and to make it even sweeter, had arrived on my mother's birthday as well.

CHAPTER TEN
THE SHOW

3 yellow pills
by Liz Holzemer

a Walgreens' vial stares at me from across the room
its contents await patiently
as the appointed hour looms
against the white kitchen counter
yellow pills stare up at me
pleading and begging to swallow all three

their chalky taste make a promise again
of electric pulses not to send
i put my faith in them, i have no choice, i must
but the misfirings begin
another broken trust

neurons gather like armies of ants
agitated and angry, on and on they rant
colors become brighter, emotions out of control
my sense of being, no longer whole

please quell the fires
you said you'd stop inside my head
the thought of more of you, i absolutely dread
liar, liar, liar, you make me ill
3 nasty, chalky, little... yellow pills

Hannah had entered our hearts and our lives. Her fair skin and rose bud lips were exquisite. Her coos, her signature scent, the way she nestled under my chin during naps—everything about her was perfect. I held her even closer to me in the early hours of September 11 as Mark and I watched in horror as the World Trade Towers came crashing down. So many lives lost and how blessed we were to have our Hannah.

It was finally *my* turn to announce her new arrival to the world. I shot roll after roll of film until I found just the right image that captured her magical essence...

> *Our miracle daughter has arrived...*
> *Hannah Elizabeth, September 6, 2001, 6:43 p.m.*
> *8 pounds, 3.8 ounces, 20.5 inches.*
> *—Proud parents Mark and Liz Holzemer*

As much as her joyous arrival delighted me, I felt guilty for my extreme exhaustion, which increased due to the baby's presence in my life. Yes, brain surgery had given me a preview of what it meant to be a sleep deprived zombie, but her insatiable appetite every two hours was difficult to keep pace with.

I couldn't help but wonder, where did brain surgery fatigue end, and newly-anointed-mother-sleep-deprived-nights-induced fatigue begin? Yes, I was an older mom too, but surely, I couldn't be *this* tired? Hannah spent her entire day eating and sleeping so how would I cope when she was crawling, walking, running? I did my best to cast my doubts aside and rather, embrace my growing love for my daughter.

Before long, it was time for our entire family to leave for Tucson, Arizona, for what would be Mark's last spring training. He had signed a one-year contract with the Arizona Diamondbacks, triple-A affiliate, the Tucson Sidewinders. Seven years into our baseball marriage, we would finally participate in family picture day and Mark could bring Hannah into the locker room after the games like the other dads did.

One afternoon while Hannah and I were napping, a strange,

somewhat familiar feeling overcame me. Was I dreaming? The bizarre sensations began deep within the depths of my very core. Tingling traveled from my toes and rose like a wave gathering momentum before it crashes upon the shore. My senses became askew with my surroundings as furniture began to sway back and forth. I shut my eyes tightly in the vain hope it would all stop. Colors grew in vibrancy and intensity. I was convinced the comforter had a life of its own as the concentric patterns sprang to life like an out of control carousel. As I had done on numerous occasions before, I looked at my watch to track the duration of the odd feeling—about thirty seconds had passed. And then I collapsed with the overwhelming fatigue I knew all too well—I'd had a partial seizure.

I tried to reassure myself it had to be attributed to the emotional highs and lows bestowed upon a new mom, and was the toll all moms had to pay. And of course, I had to be overreacting to allow the notion that "possible residual tumor" cells were growing in number and strength, collaborating on a retaliatory attack for their earlier eviction. I refused to believe it. I would not even mention it to Mark. How could something be real if it wasn't discussed, acknowledged, or given attention it did not merit?

But days later, while Hannah and I were making our weekly trek to Target for baby supplies, I couldn't deny what I desperately wished and thought had been forever extinguished. Those signature red carts once again raced around corner after corner. Packaged products became brighter. Even the courteous check out clerks scanned items at a furious pace. Utter despair and panic washed over me and I knew I had to grab Hannah and flee as fast as I could. I was certain my Target shopping days were over.

There was only one way to find out if what I dreaded and suspected was true—schedule an EEG.

Sensing the urgency in my voice, the scheduling assistant said I could have one by week's end. "Just make sure you sleep no more than five hours the night before," she instructed.

God, that would be easy, as Hannah had yet to sleep through the night.

Once again, I was navigating down those familiar hospital hallways, with their thick black arrows directing me to the right office. I couldn't help but think hospitals should have frequent visitor punch cards for patients like me. On your tenth punch, you are the lucky recipient of a free MRI and a year's worth of gadolinium.

After nearly thirty minutes of prep work—which included smearing smelly jelly in my hair— I was subjected to a battery of tests to assess my seizure threshold.

"Now, let me make sure there's a viable connection to each of the electrodes," the assistant said, as I braced myself for a thousand volts of electricity.

"Okay, now just try to relax and take a nap," were her final instructions.

I'd heard that before, was she kidding? Yes, I was exhausted, but being told to sleep on command, especially on your back when I was a stomach sleeper, was not going to happen.

Surprisingly though, I did doze off but was startled awake by flashing strobe lights. I'd defy anyone at this point not to have a seizure.

The EEG concluded with the tech asking me to breathe heavily and then bring my inhaling and exhaling back to normal pace. I felt like Koufax after a vigorous game of catch. It was quite comical despite the seriousness of it all. What did napping on command, annoying flashing lights, and rapid breathing have to do with invoking a seizure? I thought science had advanced past what I viewed as rudimentary exercises. That was enough mad science for one day.

The following week I received the grim results from my neurologist.

"Liz, you're having simple partial seizures again," he informed me, pointing out the spiked activity on the parchment scroll.

But how could this be? I thought the source of my seizures had been eliminated. I was assured my tumor wasn't growing back, but rather, scar tissue was the instigator of my misfiring neurons. It made sense—it had taken ten years for my brain to accommodate a foreign mass, now the last eighteen months had been spent reclaiming the vacuous space. That's a lot of scar tissue to plug up a hole.

Once again, why hadn't the *What to Expect After Brain Surgery* manual made mention of this possibility?

"But I don't want to take medication again," I cried.

"Think about your daughter. You wouldn't want to be holding her if you suddenly had a grand mal seizure," my doctor cautioned me.

No. I would never endanger Hannah's life. The thought was chilling.

"But we're only talking about my déjà vu seizures, aren't we?" I asked.

"Yes, we are," he replied, "but I've seen it happen in patients who've never even had a seizure before."

I knew the neurologist was right, but I was still steaming. Hadn't my intruder derived enough satisfaction beating me down the first time? Then, the second setback and now the third.

I remembered the all too familiar side effects from AEDs. The sluggishness. The fatigue. Having to remember to take my twice-daily pills. Was there something else I could try? Vitamins? Herbal remedies? I'd seek out a Shaman or voodoo doctor if possible. Why not? I'd already experimented with a batch of pills.

"There's no simple magic drug for everyone," my neurologist said. "You could try any number of newer ones that have had fairly good results."

I was thankful I had just stopped nursing and I wouldn't have to worry about harming Hannah.

Later that night, I swallowed my first dose of three nasty, chalky, little yellow pills.

CHAPTER ELEVEN
BENCHED

If you come to a fork in the road, take it.—**Yogi Berra**

It's not the disability that defines you, it's how you deal with the challenges the disability presents you with. We have an obligation to the abilities we DO have, not the disability.
  —**Jim Abbott**

When you're in a slump, it's almost as if you look out at the field and it's one big glove.—**Vance Law**

And so began my days as I ended them, with a glass of water and the pale yellow pills—my defense against the marauding army in my head. I downed them even before I kissed Mark, scooped Hannah out of her crib, made breakfast. I resented their presence in my life; a life I had diligently worked my ass off to regain the last two years. Wasn't the tumor enough punishment? Now I had the daily reminders of my prior tenant like an ex-boyfriend's favorite threadbare T-shirt left behind.

Some days the fatigue brought on by my anti-seizure medication was too much to endure. How do you explain to your thriving, energetic one-year-old daughter that you are too tired to take her on a twenty-minute walk to the park? Or that even the alternative—packing the car and driving—was too draining and bothersome, that taking a nap had greater appeal?

And what about my writing? I had scored a freelance coup, er, rather a major victory by writing regularly for a national woman's magazine but, depending on the vagaries of my energy levels, I often had to utilize the two-week option to complete an assignment generously offered by my editor.

Or how about always going to the early movie shows because I was too tired after sunset and found it difficult to focus. Then of course, there was the issue of sex. You can only knock back your spouse so many times.

PMS.
Too tired.
Not in the mood.
I have a headache.

Oops, scratch that—I hadn't had a headache since surgery. And now those damn yellow pills, Trileptal, had become excuse #22. How could 900 milligrams—truly a small dose— kill my libido as well? I was in my thirties, at the peak of my primordial urges. The Trilep had put a hex on sex.

My medicated moods ruled all aspects of my life. I was embarrassed by my own self-pity. If only I could adopt the athletic mantra of sucking it up.

"What's wrong, hun?" Mark asked one night in bed as I tried to muffle my cries of frustration and exasperation into the comforter. I wasn't feeling very comforted at all.

"Oh, it's nothing. I'm okay," I mumbled.

"Liz, Liz come on." Mark wasn't fooled by my attempted cover up.

His concern unleashed the floodgates. I turned my swollen eyes to his then burrowed into his chest. I don't remember how long my body heaved. The sobs diminished in intensity until I felt ready to speak.

"I'm tired of being tired," I finally managed to eke out. "I know I should be grateful for being alive and having Hannah, but when does this brain tumor shit stop?"

Mark wiped away my tears.

"You have to stop beating yourself up over this Liz," he said. "You're here."

Yes, he had a point, but that wasn't *my* point. This brain tumor had permeated every pore of my existence and now whatever damage it had done upstairs was taking center stage. I wished it had taken its lingering business elsewhere. My God, wasn't a decade's residence long enough?

It's over, I shouted. *We're over. Done. Fini. Kaput. Get out. Vamonos. Leave me alone.*

I tried not to give the tumor's aftermath any more thought, but despite my best efforts, I became increasingly fixated by it. This brain tumor business was nasty stuff. Not only had it destroyed a part of me physically, it had insidiously weaved its being into my very existence. I was convinced residual tumor was slowly infiltrating cell by cell, neuron by neuron, feeling by feeling.

Was it just me or is this how all brain tumor survivors feel? Why couldn't I just feel grateful for being alive? I truly was, but there was something more to all of this. Was I losing my grip on reality or was it just my own medicated-induced-fuzzy perception that I was? I grappled to grapple.

I had surgery number one. Followed not long after by surgery number two. I recovered. I became pregnant. I moved to Japan. Returned home. Had Hannah. Mark retired. It had been nearly three years, but I'd been so focused on surviving the surgeries and recovering, I hadn't taken the time to nurture my needs nor had I acknowledged the emotional impact this would have on every aspect of my life.

I'd had enough of *Get over it already.* Or *Be thankful you didn't have chemo or radiation.* True, but I was battling invisible deficits, which sometimes can be worse. But try explaining that to the non-brain tumor world. It's a losing argument when others around you minimize your side effects.

"This isn't easy stuff," Vivian reminded me during one of our phone calls, which were usually about our adjustment to motherhood. With Hannah and her daughter, Cozette, just four months apart, we enjoyed the weekly reprieve to discuss our daughters' development, endless errands and of course, what I relished most, Vivian's fashion forecast. She had a natural knack and eye for the latest on-the-horizon trends.

"I know, I know the proverbial dead horse is dead," I conceded to Viv. "I just wish I could explain to you what it feels like to be me. This isn't the same tired as being child-sleep-deprived tired."

"Are you still feeding your soul?" Vivian asked, her question a reference to the beautiful letter she'd written me during the weeks she took care of me after surgery. I was writing and spending as much time outdoors as possible. That counted didn't it?

"Yes mom." I dutifully replied.

"Izza Wizza!" Viv fired back, pulling me into line.

In all seriousness, I knew how much Vivian cared and she knew me pretty well. After all, we'd been best friends since grade school. But she hadn't had a brain tumor. I felt guilty for subconsciously punishing her for this as I did everyone else in my life who was brain tumor-less.

Maybe it *was* me and my mindset. The sooner I got over my tumor talk, the better off I'd be. I knew Prozac and Paxil weren't the answer. I also knew I didn't want to discuss my feelings with a tumor-less professional in a degree decorated office. However, I did recognize that my emotions were bubbling to the surface and I needed some type of intervention. I had to address what I'd long neglected—just how I'd go about tackling that was my next challenge. It was time to stop being a bench warmer.

CHAPTER TWELVE
FIELD OF DREAMS

To achieve great things in this world you must be able to adjust to what is being asked.—**Jim Abbott**

The difference between the impossible and the possible lies in a man's determination.—**Tommy Lasorda**

Every day is a new opportunity. You can build on yesterday's success or put its failures behind and start over again. That's the way life is, with a new game every day, and that's the way baseball is.—**Bob Feller**

I was off the bench. I had no control over my tumor. Yes, it had changed my life in the most dramatic of ways, but it didn't own me. Why continue to lament what I couldn't go back into time and prevent? I couldn't alter the diagnosis so what was I going to do with it? Mark and I had had these conversations before in a similar vein.

"When I've got a batter 0-2 on fastballs, the last thing I'm going to do is throw him another fastball. I'm going to go after him with a slider, a curve ball, a change up."

Mark was absolutely right. Change it up. Baseball, and what I now referred to as my brain tumor journey, were eerily similar. Okay, so I'd struck out a few times, been sent back to the minors, and been issued my walking papers. But slowly the message was sinking in to my probed and rearranged noggin—it wasn't a death sentence. What I'd regarded as the end of the life Liz once knew was actually the beginning of something new. Bigger. Better. My brain tumor had pitched me a life sentence.

But it still had its empty and lonely moments. Not long after my epiphany, I read about a brain tumor conference coming to town. Maybe I needed to be in the company of others like myself.

"I think it would be really great for you to go," Mark said, encouraging me.

"Caregivers are welcome too," I smiled, already knowing the answer to my not so subtle hinting.

"I personally don't need to hear a zillion stories or see other people like you Liz," Mark said. "I lived it. You're here, that's enough for me."

It was up to me then to make the foray into unchartered territory alone. Naturally, I was apprehensive. What's a brain tumor conference all about anyway? I would soon find out.

The weekend conference, while empowering, was also overwhelming. I felt an instant affinity with those whose upside-down question mark scars resembled mine. They were all too common on freshly shaved, shiny skulls. Foolish me thinking Dr. Fullagar had personalized my cranium with a tattoo as unique as myself. Maybe he should seek out a patent to prevent copyright infringement.

The welcoming address, laden with medical terminology, soared right over my head. Judging by the expressions on many faces, I could tell others felt the same. I had a hard time processing terms and statistics that for the most part had little or no relevance to me. But the pièce de résistance was a Power-Point presentation packed with gory tumor resection pictures. Image after image flashing before my eyes just about did me in. Even though I'd only sparingly indulged from the breakfast buffet, I felt it making its way back up my throat. There was nowhere to hide, so I shielded my eyes until it was over.

"That really didn't do me any good," I heard one attendee mumble. Then, "I just want to know how to get through each day," from another. Or "How is this supposed to help me now?" The general consensus was that confusing jargon and confronting pictures were of little benefit to us. Had I attended such a conference before my own surgery, my fear factor meter would have rocketed off the scale.

However, I found the specific topic sessions valuable—especially the ones focusing on seizures now that they had been reintroduced to my reality. But again, there was so much information presented—my brain went into overdrive and nearly crashed my system.

Most surprising and somewhat disconcerting to me were the strategically placed display tables one had to navigate around to attend the different sessions. The way the smartly dressed representatives manned their tables promoting their latest products, made me feel as if I were attending an auto trade show. Beautifully appointed booths might just as well have had signs proclaiming:

> Cyberknife—one zap and your tumor is gone!
> Killing tumors one zap at a time!
> Our drugs don't leave you feeling drugged out.
> The only time-release wafer proven to kill tumor cells.
> Melts in your brain, not in your mouth.

Now I'd seen it all—drug and tumor removal advertorial promos. There was even competition within the brain tumor community.

My biggest disappointment was lunch—the tables were arranged according to tumor type and you were encouraged to sit with your similarly afflicted tumor sufferers. We were categorized by the tumor we'd never asked or wanted to have bestowed upon us. I scanned the room for the meningioma table, but only noticed white linen covered ones for astrocytomas, glioblastomas, oligodendrogliomas...the really nasty tumors. I asked a server where meningiomas belonged. She shrugged her shoulders. Then I saw a table with a placard that said *Benign*.

"May I sit here?" I asked a group of women. "I'm a meningioma."

"Yes, yes, please," they encouraged. "We're meningiomas too."

I had a lunch date, but I was peed off that we were regarded as so insignificant we had been lumped together under the benign blanket—we didn't even merit our own table.

The highlight of the conference was meeting others like me. Some had had surgery, others had just learned of their diagnosis and were searching for the Holy Grail. From what I gathered, of those with meningioma, I appeared to be the youngest. Most were women in their forties and fifties. Nevertheless, I was face to face with my own people, flock if you will.

I packed up my multi-sponsored canvas tote bag filled with more informational brochures and gimmicky souvenirs— drug sponsored pens and magnets— than I cared to own, and headed home.

During the drive home, I felt more confused than before and a nagging feeling kept bothering me. What was the source of my conference confusion? Too much disseminated information to process? Feeling snubbed because it seemed I didn't have the "right" type of tumor? My inability to understand the issues people with other types of tumors had? Or all of the above?

Subconsciously, however, seeds were being planted. As I continued to go about my days raising Hannah and writing, something was beginning to take hold of me. And then came the knock on my door—

It was my neighbor. I was taken aback by the pained look of concern in his eyes, and the reason behind it was far more serious than I could have ever expected.

"Liz, tell me everything you know about a meningioma," he said, words slowly forming.

"Why? What's wrong?" I asked, my voice shaking.

"I have one," he blurted out.

The hairs on the back of my neck stood on end. Were we really having this conversation? How could this be? We were neighbors and this was too close for comfort.

"Oh my God! Oh my God!" I kept repeating under my breath in disbelief.

Within minutes I learned that my neighbor had a massive meningioma like I'd had and it was dangerously located between his eyes. And, like mine, the tumor was life threatening, surgery would be risky, and he was seeking the same information I'd scrambled to find when I had first heard those four life-altering words.

I was stunned. What were the odds of someone living in my suburban tract—let alone across the street—being afflicted with a brain tumor? And—not only that—but a *meningioma* to boot!

Over the next few days, I tried to guide my neighbor and his family along the unchartered map and foreign terrain of his brain tumor journey. Whereas on my journey I had no control over or knowledge of what I was embarking upon, now I had the passport, map, and itinerary to share so he wouldn't feel quite as alone and fearful about his unknown destination as I had. What a tremendous and hugely gratifying feeling it was for me.

Then unbelievably, not long after another neighbor told me *he'd* been diagnosed with several brain tumors, one of them *also* a meningioma. Okay, now this was getting just plain scary.

I couldn't escape the brain tumor curse. Were brain tumors caused or diagnosed simply by association? Would I soon become a neighborhood pariah? Never mind a flu epidemic or mumps' outbreak. Soon neighbors would issue warnings— "Watch out for that Liz—she's a walking, living, breathing brain tumor contagion." I began to wonder whether I should voluntarily quarantine myself. But deep down inside I knew that was just nonsense.

Was I suddenly more aware of them because I was a survivor? Or had they been around all along and I only began to notice them because of my own diagnosis? How many others were out there feeling as isolated and helpless as I had?

It seemed no matter where I was, either I met someone with a brain tumor or someone knew of a brother whose sister-in-law's co-worker's boss' next-door neighbor had one.

It had become the six degrees of brain tumor.

I soon learned by dealing with my survivor status in an open and humorous way, I could break down the stigma involved with brain tumor deficits, as well as find other survivors in the most unlikely of places. Whether enjoying lunch solo and asking the waitress to warn me of any food plastered to my numb face because I couldn't feel it, or forgetting my PIN number and joking with the Safeway clerk that it was my damn brain tumor again only to have her say, "You may be joking, but I did have a brain tumor!" to which I replied, "Believe me I wasn't joking," I never missed an opportunity to raise the brain tumor bar.

I needed to discuss my feelings with someone who would understand. Family and friends were supportive, but it wasn't their fault they couldn't help me break in my new shoes. I knew it was time to attend a support group. Because I wasn't a person who shares her most intimate feelings to a room full of strangers, I wasn't completely sold on the idea, but decided to try one on for size. One extremely positive and unexpected outcome of multiple brain surgeries was my new no-holds-barred attitude towards life, that nothing could scare me anymore. When you've had your skull cracked open, pieces of it soaked in a petri dish for hours, then magically pieced and stitched back together, well, not much else could really traumatize you.

I attended a few support groups and initially only listened. But soon I found myself nodding in agreement and chiming in with my own first-hand accounts. The drawback to the support groups was the locale—they were usually held on hospital grounds. Yes, it was great to talk to people branded by the same battle scars, but the setting just didn't do it for me. The familiar stench, glaring fluorescent lights, reliving the fear all over again—it was too much. Why voluntarily return to the scene of the crime when I had to revisit it anyway for annual MRIs, exams, and EEGs? I wanted to connect to others in a friendlier environment, one devoid of the painful reminders of the day we faced the greatest horror in our lives. I wanted something on tap, especially on the bad days when I didn't have the energy to drive or felt a breakthrough seizure coming on. A safe refuge, but in the privacy and comfort of my own home. Just like my freelance writing—if I had to, I could finish up my assignments and just click *send* from my computer.

Eureka! From my computer...that was it. What if I built a virtual cyberspace community? Chat rooms were popular for dating, dispensing new motherhood advice or searching for recipes, so why not a cranium chatroom? Bang, this was my Oprah *a-ha* moment!

I made a quick call.

"Vivi, are you free for lunch?"

"What's up, Liz?" she asked.

"I have an idea and I need your help".

"Yes, let's go!"

I loved Vivi's spontaneity—if I called or shouted over the fence for a quick diversion, she always had the time for a chat.

We packed up Hannah and headed to one of our favorite salad buffets. During the quick drive, I broke the news about my idea.

"I want to create a forum for people like me," I explained. "A safe haven for those on the brain tumor journey."

"Oh Lizzy, it sounds divine!" she said. "I can't wait to hear more over lunch."

Vivi gave me her full attention as I shared my vision of building a brain tumor sanctuary.

"What if I shared my own story and provided a place for others to do the same? People could ask the questions I had wanted to ask and get the answers I couldn't get."

Hannah babbled back at me, seemingly in agreement with my brilliant idea. I knew I was on the right track if even my own daughter approved.

"I think it's brilliant!" Vivi said, following Hannah's lead. "How will you do it?"

"That's where I'm stuck," I admitted.

I needed a catchy name—something distinctive to set me apart from all the other support services that existed out there.

"Liz, you're the writer. How about a play on words or something along those lines?" Vivi said.

Now we were onto something. I'd always complained about how difficult it was to pronounce the name of my tumor, let alone spell it. So why not make it the focal point so *no one* could ever forget what it was. And I couldn't overlook the obvious—this was primarily a women's disease as well.

Meningioma. Mmm. Meningioma Moments. I still seemed to have quite a few of those on a weekly basis. Meningioma what, hmm. I had another flashback to the day when my fate was sealed. That was exactly my reaction then. A meningioma "what?" was right!

I also remembered the first call I made—to my mother. Mom. Or Momma, as I call her when we embrace each other tightly. "Ah, Momma." And she always replies back, "Momma loves you."

"That's it!" I yelled, nearly choking on the Greek salad.

Meningioma Mommas. I had my catchy name.

Vivi pushed a clean serviette toward me.

"Scribble it down for posterity so you'll always remember when your dream first took hold of you," she encouraged.

I jotted down the name and then started to think about what graphics might go along with it. But writing was my forte, not artistic design.

"How about something simple?" If my target audience was going to be those who had trouble concentrating or difficulty focusing as I still did, I needed to make it easy. Just like the first rule of journalism school. KISS: Keep It Simple Stupid.

I doodled three female stick figures with outstretched arms and frazzled hair. Under the first one I wrote *hope*; the second, *friendship*; and the last, *laughter.*

"I've got it!" I said, waving my design in the air.

In celebration, Vivi and I clinked our glasses of pink lemonade against Hannah's sippee cup.

"Cheers!" Hannah cheered.

I'd taken my final warm up swing in the on deck circle and was now making my way to the plate.

CHAPTER THIRTEEN
OPENING DAY

A life is not important except in the impact it has on other lives.—**Jackie Robinson**

Find something you love, and go after it, with all of your heart.—**Jim Abbott**

Set your goals high, and don't stop till you get there.
  —**Bo Jackson**

I had a game plan. Now that I'd been granted a second chance at life, I knew what I wanted do with it. I'd given birth to Hannah, now it was time to give birth to my brain child—Meningioma Mommas.

My dream was to create a forum where I could share my story while giving hope and encouragement to others. I wanted an alternative to numbers, percentages, and grim statistics—there were already enough of those discouraging places out there as I quickly discovered when I was diagnosed. Besides, why should a number define a person's prognosis and recovery? And I wanted to share my message that you have to trust your body's signals, instincts, and inner voice as I had done.

I decided to go through a web site developer Mark had been

using for his own business. I had my vision—I just needed to somehow communicate it to my design team.

They fired off questions quicker than I could deflect. Their first criticism was the name.

What's a meningioma momma?
Hold on, we can't even say that!
Have you thought about how difficult it will be to find you in a search engine?
No one will even know how to spell that.

"Wouldn't it be easier if you just called it BRAINTUMOR-BABES.COM?" they suggested. "It certainly would be simpler for people to find you."

"Oh, puleeze," I cringed, imagining testosterone-fired-up males confusing my site for a soft-porn website. Only mine would have fully-clad women who tastefully exposed their surgical scars. I could see it now—Frontal Lobe Frannie enjoys long walks, romantic dinners but no wine please—they trigger her seizures; Sally Sphenoid Wing is looking for a man with deep pockets since she's on disability; Pamela Parasagittal prefers quiet evenings at home—she has a low tolerance for noise since surgery.

Ah, the joys of working with a male web development team.

"You're such naysayers," I joked with them, and we all enjoyed a good laugh. Yep, my sense of humor was still intact.

But I was prepared for their criticisms, put my game face on, and set them straight.

I'm a meningioma momma! This was my defiant, kick-ass way of shouting to the world, *Despite you, you, meningioma, I still became a mom. And guess what? I'm still a wife, a daughter, a friend, a sister-in-law, a writer—I can perform all these roles and wear multiple hats.*

And trust me, if you've been diagnosed with a meningioma,

you will quickly learn how to spell it as well as pronounce it.

I also wanted Meningioma Mommas to battle the so-called "benign" brain tumor stigma. Meningiomas are the most prevalent primary brain tumor and I was tired of them being overlooked. It was akin to being the most popular kid at school yet being the wallflower at the school dance—neglected and passed over. We needed a dance of our own.

Over the ensuing weeks, my dream of a twenty-four seven online non-profit support group took shape. It would be one-stop shopping at its best—the Super Target of brain tumor shopping experiences. Just as I enjoy shopping for diapers, reasonably priced clothes, and groceries under the same roof, Meningioma Mommas would offer the same great customer service with cerebral contacts, hemispheric happenings, and tumor humor. Yes, what woman wouldn't want to laugh, cry, and vent, all the while connecting with others wearing the same shoes?

Now I just had to figure out a way to deliver the message that Meningioma Mommas existed.

Using my journalistic background—see, Mom & Dad, all those years of college did pay off!—I wrote press release after press release bombarding the Denver media as well as every other national media outlet I could Google an address for. I wrote to news shows, talk shows, radio shows. I sent emails, made calls, left messages. Surely someone had to respond.

But nothing. Not a single bite. Those who were kind enough to reply to me, proffered the standard rejection line *"Although your organization sounds interesting, we're just not covering brain tumors."* And no one was interested in writing about an online chat room for a tumor they'd never heard of. Of course not, brain tumors weren't sexy or glamorous. Slighted again. They failed to see all the essential, heartstring-pulling story elements in place:

Good looking major league ball player.
Throw in a smart California blonde wife.
He throws strikes for a living.
She grows a baseball-sized brain tumor.
See baseball and baseball?

My own profession frustrated me at times. To say I was disappointed was a huge understatement, but despite the lack of publicity, and after a three month gestation period, I planned to go live with Meningioma Mommas in February 2003. It seemed the appropriate time as it would coincide with my three-year "second chance" anniversary month.

But they say timing is everything. I was flabbergasted when one day Mark called me from work.

"Hey hun, you'll never believe this, but a producer from the *Today Show* emailed the Arizona Diamondbacks trying to track us down," Mark relayed to me.

"What do they want? What did they say?" I asked, with growing excitement.

"They wanted to know if the Diamondbacks would release our email address and phone number to them," Mark continued.

"You said yes of course, right?" I hoped.

"Hold on, I'm emailing you all the information right now."

Apparently the same letter I'd written months ago to the various magazines recounting my second chance story had fallen into the lap of an interested producer.

I couldn't believe it. One phone call later and the *Today Show* had set up a shooting schedule.

I had to admit it was exciting—journalism was my chosen field and now it was *my* story being told instead of me telling someone else's. I was realistic though—filming a story didn't necessarily guarantee a run date. A late breaking story could change all that.

But it didn't and my segment aired in the second hour on February 25, 2003. Vivian was the first to call.

"Izza Wizza!" she screamed. "The story was great and I cried when I saw you all. It brought back such memories."

"Thanks Viv, I can't wait to see it," I said.

I still had an hour before it would air in Mountain Standard Time.

I paced the floors until I heard Katie Couric's familiar voice, "This morning on Today's health—brain tumors...For one Colorado woman, it was her own gut feeling that may have saved her life."

And then it was show time.

Tears streamed down my face as I clutched Hannah against my chest and relived the journey that brought her into my life.

"They did a really beautiful job," Mark said, hugging the two of us, teary-eyed himself.

It didn't take long before the supportive calls and messages from family and friends flowed in:

We're so proud of you.

What were you and Mark mumbling under your breaths?

Hannah's a TV ham!

You didn't look nervous at all.

We had no idea that's what you went through.

Not only these, but my website received thousands of hits and a tidal wave of emails poured in from people affected by or suffering from a meningioma, just like me. I was surprised my Outlook Express and website didn't sink from all the traffic! Total strangers poured out their feelings through wrenching emails and letters.

"I had no idea someone else felt like I did. Thank you for sharing your story. Now I know I am not alone."

"Hello Liz. I was also diagnosed with a rare brain tumor two years ago. Being so young, it came as quite a shock. I have tried for several years to have children, but unfortunately have been unsuccessful. Your story has inspired me to let me

know there is a chance. In the past two years, I have had two brain surgeries along with several health difficulties. It is hard for others to realize what a trauma something like this can be. It is nice to know there is hope. Thank you so much for the inspiration."

"I am so glad things are going great for you and that you are healthy. I am going through things that when I was watching you it sounded soooo like me. I am scared. I am happy to know that with what you have gone through, there is hope."

"I was recently diagnosed with a meningioma in January of this year. I was scared out of my mind. Just three weeks ago from today, I was in the hospital undergoing neurosurgery to have it removed. I thought I was the only one in the country who had this. I had never heard of it before. I was so embarrassed to talk to anyone about this. I didn't want anyone to know. Thank you."

"I saw your story on the Today Show this morning and could completely relate to you. I hurried to the computer and here I am! It is so wonderful to find a site that deals with this issue."

"Liz, you are a star! Walk of Fame! Grammy nomination! But no encore performances...please. Seriously though, what a very touching and heart felt story—even more so that I have had the pleasure of getting to know you and your family. Your story deserves the attention it received. You are a walking miracle and I do believe that you are truly blessed. It is my belief that all life events happen for a reason. We may not know at the time but the Universe has a way to bring them to light and when that light shines, the world can truly change for the better. You, without a doubt, are in that light!"

I had gone out on a limb and people were responding. I couldn't have asked for a better Opening Day.

CHAPTER FOURTEEN
LIL' LEAGUER

No one wants to hear about the labor pains, they just want to see the baby.—**Lou Brock**

There are only two ways to live your life. One is as though nothing is a miracle. The other is as though everything is a miracle.—**Albert Einstein**

The new team in town was a hit. It was hard to find an empty seat in the stadium with new players joining every day. Not only that, word quickly spread past America's borders and my second family had truly become multicultural and diverse with members from Australia to Zimbabwe. I felt as if I'd scored the winning home run.

While Meningioma Mommas continued to grow in numbers, so did my freelance writing assignments. Whenever a story landed on my editor's desk about a brain-related condition, she called me immediately and I soon became the in-house expert on the subject. I knew the relevant questions to ask because I lived with the answers every day.

My doubts about ever writing again had finally been put to rest. Not only had I reinvented myself, but I'd also relaunched my writing career with an entirely new platform of experience to draw upon. Who knew a brain tumor had *this* advantage?

That summer, Mark, Hannah, and I attended the Holzemer family reunion. Held every five years on the original and still operating Holzemer Homestead in Amidon, North Dakota, it was a relaxing Fourth of July weekend of reminiscing, meeting new cousins, eating, and of course, watching the excellently choreographed forty-five minute fireworks display.

The reunion, however, was tinged with great sadness as the previous fall, we had lost Mark's father to cancer. Harold—or Big Red as he was otherwise known—was loved just as much for his bigger than life presence as he was for his corny jokes, narrative storytelling, and competitive Scrabble games. I had never known anyone else who could come up with a three-letter word earning triple points.

On our drive back home on two-lane roads past miles of cornfields, Mark was unusually quiet.

"Let's have another baby," he suddenly blurted out.

I was taken aback.

"Oh hun, we were lucky to have Hannah," I said. "And I don't think we could be *that* lucky again."

"I want a son," Mark continued, nudging me. "I want to be a father to a son the way my dad was to me."

His eyes welled up. No matter how stern Mark came across at times, his tough-as-nails athletic exterior often gave way to allow the most sensitive guy in the world to emerge.

As much as it broke my heart to see Mark yearning for another child, deep down inside I felt uneasy. After all, I wasn't getting any younger and I'd learned a lot more about the risks of having children with my brain tumor history. Anything that could fuel growth in any lurking residual tumor cells was a risk and many doctors believed, as I did, that hormones played a starring role in the growth of meningiomas. In fact, my roommate was classified as progesterone receptive and I had already been warned that HRT was out of the question for me when the dreaded menopause years arrived. So who knew what effect rampant pregnancy hormones could have on my NO VACANCY sign, not to mention my seizure threshold?

Having grown up with three younger brothers, a part of me felt tremendous sadness that Hannah might be sibling-less. If she was, I just hoped she wouldn't grow up and accuse me of depriving her of a brother or sister. It was a miracle I'd had her and I honestly believed Hannah was the only one I'd been allotted. Could we tempt fate again?

The decision of whether or not to pursue expanding our family weighed heavily on my mind. I couldn't help but replay the internal debate each day.

Not long after my thirty-sixth birthday, an overwhelming fatigue stopped me in my tracks. Even allowing for how busy my life was raising Hannah and running my growing non-profit, I was gassed. I was three days late too. Ever since my cycles had returned post surgery, I had been as regular as clockwork.

"Nah couldn't be," I joked to Vivian. "Could it?"

"We do become more fertile as we age," Vivian pointed out.

Too nervous to tell Mark my suspicions in case I was wrong, I took a pregnancy test, and then another. Both revealed the double blue lines confirming what I truly believed was impossible. There was only one way to find out for sure.

I scheduled an appointment with my ob-gyn and she congratulated me again—I was going to give Hannah a brother or sister after all.

"Um, hun, you are not going to believe this," I told Mark that evening.

"Now what?" Mark wondered, accustomed to the many unpleasant surprises in our life.

"Remember that conversation we had on the way back from the reunion last month?" I asked. "Well, you're going to be a dad again!" I squealed in delight.

It was déjà vu—without the need to take extra meds—with the initial surprise and shock followed by tears of joy.

The euphoria, however, was short-lived by the harsh realities of my predicament. I couldn't help but worry about the dangers, side effects, and potential irrevocable damage AEDs could have upon a developing fetus. I became a self-obsessed Google geek searching for the answers I so desperately sought. But the information was confusing, conflicting, and left me feeling in a greater quandary than before. Were they harmful? Harmless? Instead of a nurturing, umbilical cord lifeline, was I gradually snuffing out the life that I fought to develop? The AEDs had already knocked the socks off me, so what were they were doing to my son or daughter?

During the weeks that followed, I often broke down in tears tormented by what I should do. I was medication-free during Hannah's pregnancy and now I was exposing my developing baby to those goddamn chalky pills, not once, but twice a day. Would I also cause my baby irreparable neurological damage?

My team of doctors—high risk, ob-gyn, neurologist—all reassured me that I was on a low dosage, and many, many epileptic women like myself took much higher doses of AEDs yet still had normal, healthy babies. I was repeatedly told the risks to my baby of completely stopping my medication far outweighed those, if any, of staying on them. I could have a grand mal seizure and not only harm the baby, but myself as well. Was I, as a mother-to-be of two, foolish enough to take that risk? Absolutely not, but the added burden of doubt was unshakable.

"Liz, Hannah is perfectly healthy," Mark kept reminding me. "And this baby will be too."

"But I'm the one carrying the baby," I sobbed. "I'm the one responsible who is supposed to give our child a head start in life."

A few weeks later, I had the first of many ultrasounds. Having Mark accompany me allayed most of my growing concerns and fears.

"Do you want to know the sex of the baby?" the doctor asked.

"Of course!" we said in unison.

I'd always said that with my children I had to know. And it was critical to find out if I'd be painting the nursery blue or pink.

As she slathered cool jelly over my belly, Mark and I anxiously awaited the news of whether Hannah would become a big sister to a brother or sister.

"A fast, strong heartbeat," the doctor announced.

Hannah's heartbeat had been fast and strong, too. Another daughter?

"Limbs and organs look good," she continued.

Good, my baby had all its parts.

The baby was tightly tucked in like a roly poly. Then it untucked its legs.

"Are you sure you want to know?" she asked again.

"Yes!" we shouted.

"It's a boy!"

Mark's wish on the Holzemer Homestead had come true.

However, before we could even enjoy the revelation that we were having a son, the doctor punctured our proud-as-punch-parent moment by informing us our son had ultrasound markers. What the hell were markers? We'd never heard of them before. We didn't even have to ask the question before she went on to explain that the presence of these markers could be an indication that our son had chromosomal abnormalities, meaning he could be born with certain deficits. Or they could be innocuous and he would be born perfectly healthy. The only way to know was to schedule an amniocentesis, "especially in light of your age," she just had to add.

Was it me or was the room spinning? I couldn't tell the difference. I needed to lie down—wait, I already was. Could anything ever be easy for me? Just once, please.

Yes, I was thirty-six, but only two years ago, I'd had a perfectly healthy, complication-free pregnancy with Hannah, and now my age had become more of a detrimental factor than my brain tumor history.

We were then forewarned of the risks—oh goody as if I hadn't already weathered enough of those in my three plus decades of life—of having an amniocentesis. The greatest risk being that one in two hundred resulted in abortion. And to add insult to injury, we had to act soon otherwise I'd miss the window of opportunity based on how far along I was.

Once again, during the drive home, Mark and I were the stunned, silenced husband and wife. The fear was palpable, and all too familiar.

"So what do you think of Dr. Death?" Mark asked, finally breaking the silence.

I couldn't help but chuckle.

"On one hand, I'm told I'm going to have a son, yet before I can even savor the moment, I'm then told he could have a host of birth defects," Mark continued.

I didn't say a word. He needed to get that off his chest.

In the days that followed, we kept going back and forth about what we should do.

I called, emailed, and questioned every girlfriend I knew who was a mom. Pros and cons of amnio? What would you do if this were your baby? I needed guidance, hope, reassurance that the decision I had to make was the right one. But I knew that ultimately no one could decide for me—only I could.

Call it mother's intuition. Maternal instinct. What you will. Days later, I woke up with the answer as clear as day. In my heart, I knew what I had to do so I rang the doctor before I had second thoughts.

"I've decided to have the amnio," I told the receptionist.

"Come in right now," she instructed. "Once our patients

have made up their minds, we like them to come in as quickly as possible before they have a change of heart."

I called Mark at work and told him I was on my way to pick him up.

"You need to take the rest of the day off as I have strict orders to stay off my feet after the test," I relayed to him.

"Not a problem," he said. "Are you sure you want to do this Liz? What about the pain?"

"Mark, that's the least of my worries. I know I avoid needles, but really. What's a needle in a belly compared to skill saws and titanium screws in a cranium? I won't rest easy until I know our son is okay," I said, surer than I'd ever been about anything before in my life.

In the end, the procedure was painless—nothing more than a momentary sting.

We were told we'd have the test results in a few weeks.

Mark took me home and I spent the rest of the day on the couch, taking it easy per doctor's orders.

A week earlier than we expected, the doctor called. I braced for the worst. After all, I was accustomed to doomsday phone calls.

"Your son has forty-six chromosomes," she said.

I assumed that was a good thing.

"This means no missing chromosomes," she explained.

My heart stopped racing. Simply stated, chromosomal abnormalities could be ruled out. However, for other reasons my pregnancy was still classified as high risk and I continued to be closely monitored.

As I began to slow down and grow wearier, I handed over the Meningioma Momma reins to my Executive Director, Lindy Klarenbeek, who lived in Australia. Lindy had joined Meningioma Mommas on behalf of her aunt who'd been diagnosed with seven meningiomas. After experiencing firsthand the wonderful support her aunt received, and appreciating the value of such a forum, she generously offered to become involved with its administration.

Naps now became a daily part of my routine. Sweet Hannah was very accommodating and quite intuitive for her two years.

"Now mommy, you rest," she often ordered me, pointing to the bed of blankets she would arrange on the living room couch. She was the perfect big sister in the making.

While Jacob's—the name we had tentatively agreed upon— impending arrival approached without further complications, I received another unexpected surprise. However, this one didn't send me into panic mode. *Woman's Day* had emailed me. Could it be that one of my freelance story proposals had finally garnered the attention of a top-notch editor? The thought of writing for a major New York magazine was a dream come true. Of course, I would happily accept any assignment.

But it wasn't an offer to write for *Woman's Day*; my writing hadn't been noticed at all. It was something else.

> *Dear Liz,*
>
> *As you may or may not know, Lindy Klarenbeek recently nominated you to be a recipient of our fourth annual Woman's Day Awards. The awards honor four women from across the country who reach out to their communities, better the lives of others and push themselves to extraordinary limits. In doing so, these women teach the rest of us the true meaning of courage, humanity and purpose.*
>
> *We received an overwhelming number of nominations and I am pleased to inform you have made it to the next round. To aid us in our decision we would like to know a little bit more about you. Would you please take a few minutes to fill out the attached form and return it to us? Thanks and we look forward to learning more about you!*

Please feel free to contact me with any questions.

Best, Alexa Stevenson, Woman's Day

"Oh my God!" I shouted. I grabbed Hannah and started dancing with her.

I couldn't believe it. When had Lindy done this? I had to know so, fingers shaking and totally forgetting it was 3 a.m. in Australia, I dialed her number.

"Lindy, Lindy!"

"Liz, what's up? It's three in the morning," she said, half asleep.

"Sorry, but you won't believe this," I said. "*Woman's Day* just wrote me about being in the final running for some award you nominated me for. What's this all about?"

"Fair dinkum Liz, this is fantastic!" Lindy said, quickly waking up. "If you win, it will be HUGE, all that national exposure for Meningioma Mommas. Plus there's a $5,000 award. What do you have to do?"

"Hold on, let me read it again," I offered, thinking how surreal this was and then before Lindy could even comment, "What should I write?" I asked. "I'll get started now."

"Slow down," Lindy said. "You've still got a few weeks before the baby is due. We've got plenty of time to work on it. I'm thrilled, but now I'm going back to bed. We'll savor this later."

Yes, Lindy was right, but how could I not respond as quickly as possible? Over the next few days, I reread and pondered the attached list of questions. I wanted to make sure I didn't overlook any salient points I felt needed to be included, but basically they wanted to know why I had started my non-profit and what kept me motivated. Simply put, my goal was to soften the shock of what I call the "brain tumor journey" and I was motivated every day knowing that Meningioma Mommas prevented others from feeling the same isolation, devastation, and fear I had felt when I was first diagnosed.

I'd literally just applied the finishing touches to the applica-
tion when a series of intermittent stabbing pains forced me on
all fours. It felt like the Jaws of Life clenching and unclench-
ing on my lower back. Was it? Could it possibly be? Jacob still
had another three plus weeks to roast and this felt like nothing I had experienced with Hannah.

"Breathe, Liz," I kept repeating to myself.

I placed a call to my doctor and was instructed to record
the episodes. Apparently, I could be in back labor and if the
contractions increased in frequency for more than an hour, I
should go to the hospital.

I called Mark to warn him our son could be making an
early appearance, packed my bag, and lined up all my ducks
in a row.

By late afternoon, I'd had enough.

"Mark, come home now," I begged. "I think Jacob wants out!"

As Mark sped to the hospital, I couldn't help but hope it
would be the last time I'd ever check in as a patient. Let's have
this baby and chuck out my frequent patient punch card once
and for all, I mused.

"Yes, you're having back labor," a nurse confirmed once I'd
been situated.

I could have told her that hours ago I thought to myself, gri-
macing through another contraction.

"Hurry, hit me with an epidural!" I begged.

The doctors estimated the baby would arrive just before
midnight.

"Oh please, Jacob, hold out until April Fool's," I said.

Diamond is the birthstone for April and I figured after all my
body had been through, I deserved a diamond something or
other. If need be, I'd keep my legs crossed until 12:01 a.m.

I got my wish.

After thirty-six weeks and four days, our little leaguer
arrived healthy at exactly 12:30 a.m. With that downy straw-

berry blond hair, there was only one name befitting for him.

"Hunter Harold Holzemer!" announced a proud father in tears. "Triple-H!"

I couldn't have agreed more about the name and what an ode to Big Red.

No joking, our future All-Star Hunter Harold arrived on April Fool's 2004, 6 pounds, 10 ounces, 20 inches. Welcomed with love by Mark, Liz, & Big Sis Hannah

CHAPTER 15
GRAND SLAM

My motto was always to keep swinging. Whether I was in a slump or feeling badly or having trouble off the field, the only thing to do was keep swinging.—**Hank Aaron**

Never let the fear of striking out get in your way.—**Babe Ruth**

If you ever get a second chance in life for something, you've got to go all the way.—**Lance Armstrong**

Call them the baseball clichés of all time, but I feel I own them. I had struck out swinging hard, been benched with setback after setback, released, told to pack up and go home.

I refused to give up though. I'd hit for the cycle. Rounded the bases. Pitched a perfect game. Had winning season after season.

I never thought I'd get to the point of feeling how I do today. I recall months of not being able to focus, the aggravation of constantly looking up words in the dictionary I used to know how to spell, the lack of concentration that made it difficult to read a newspaper or a book. I also remember the physical deficits—the exhaustion I felt from just taking a shower, the helplessness of not completing simple activities, and the frustration of not fully participating in the life I once had.

I'd come full circle on my brain tumor journey. A journey that took seven years to complete. The family I dreamed of and never thought possible is mine after all. The writing career I thought was over is rejuvenated and thriving. I will be on medication for the rest of my life and will always worry about the "what ifs." But I will keep stepping up to the plate and perfecting the new Liz.

How did I arrive at this place?

It's taken years of compromise, patience, and finally, acceptance to live my life as me again. As Vivian constantly reminds me: *You've reinvented yourself; your spirit has returned.* I like to think of it as the newer, improved version of the old me.

Long gone are the drab colors of my wardrobe—the grays, blues and beiges. I prefer vibrant and bolder ones now.

And I believe I'm a better mother because I'm more relaxed and don't get hung up on what I *should* be doing as a mom—I'm just thankful I *am* one.

I still marvel at the fact my silent roommate had been a part of me for over one third of my life before it decided to make its presence known. I was never one to put a lot of faith in signs, but for me personally, I credit my inner voice one hundred percent for saving my life. My inner voice, which kept nagging at me—like an exasperated wife with her "honey do list"—until I finally listened. It's easy to say in hindsight—considering all the symptoms I had—that I could have been diagnosed years sooner than I actually was. But it was not meant to be.

Never ever would I have believed that four words strung together in a simple sentence would deliver me a life I celebrate every day. And I feel multiply blessed that I have the rest of my life to make an imprint.

EPILOGUE

My life today includes loving my two miracles Hannah and Hunter and trying not to deal the "brain tumor card" to Mark.

I will continue to have yearly MRIs to monitor the suspicious area that has indicated some change. I hope that the batter in the on deck circle will stay put.

Meningioma Mommas continues to grow by several new mommas and poppas a day.

I've also established Hunter's Hope Chest in honor of my son to study the effects of AEDs during pregnancy and in breastfeeding mothers.

A portion of the sales of this book will be donated to meningioma specific research. To date, we have raised over $25,000.

By the way, I nearly forgot—call it a meningioma moment— I did win that *Woman's Day* "Women Who Inspire Us" Award and the $5,000 honorarium was donated to research.

Thank you, and please remember that you need not be alone on your journey.

ADDENDUM

There cannot be a crisis next week. My schedule is already full.—**Henry Kissinger**

If we knew what it was we were doing, it would not be called research, would it?—**Albert Einstein**

If you made it this far, I hope you will glean useful information from the following stuff I call, "What I wished I'd really been told." I wasn't, so now I'm going to tell you. Keep in mind, some of it may be relevant and work for you, some of it may not, but you'll be offered information your team of doctors usually don't have the time to provide. Their job is to save your life, mine is to equip you with the emotional and practical tips to help you cope. You can't change the diagnosis, but you can soften the shock. While some of this may sound very scary, it's like childbirth—some will breeze through it, and others will labor at it, pardon the pun.

LIZ'S BRAIN TUMOR MANUALS DEFINED

When You Have to Have Brain Surgery

- **Take a deep breath**. Take another. Okay, one more. I won't sugarcoat it—"You have a brain tumor" is most likely the scariest sentence you will hear in your lifetime. But you CAN do this and you WILL.

- **Don't be hasty** in your treatment decisions—research. Research as much as you can. Seek out a second opinion at the very least.

- **Be leery of neurosurgeons with caveman tools** and mail-order degrees hanging in their offices.

- **Make sure your living will is in order, you have power of attorney, and life directives are known in advance.** In the unfortunate circumstance you don't make it back through those double OR doors, the last thing you want to happen is for your second or third cousin to inherit your prized Bee Gees CD collection. It was a legitimate concern of mine.

- Whether you have days, weeks, or months to prepare, **do not become an obsessed Google-geek trying to find out everything there is to know about your tumor.** Everyone is different and a lot of the scary statistics and frightening facts you will unearth may not even apply to you.

- Instead of doing the above, **join a support group.** If you've been diagnosed with a meningioma, of course I highly recommend Meningioma Mommas— meningiomamommas.org. You'll get straightforward, honest answers, often with a sense of humor to boot, from compassionate survivors and those newly diagnosed. Also, ask your doctor if he or she is able to connect you with a patient in your same shoes. Even if you're wearing the wrong size, the nearly familiar fit will be more helpful than you can possibly imagine.

- Family, friends, neighbors, and everyone you've never met will try to fill your Neuro-ICU room all at once. It's the whole "let's stop and gawk at the grisly accident" phenomenon. People will want to see your head wrapped in a gauzy turban and are morbidly curious as to WHO is under the bandages NOW.

- Without being too graphic, let's just say the hospital hash will only add to your already Decadron-fueled backed-up bogs. Trust me, when it was finally time for me to extricate a week's worth of slop, I nearly re-split myself open while writhing at the base of my porcelain god. **Ask family members to sneak in food**. Anything with Dairy Queen emblazoned across it works too. And stock up on the Colace.

- **You will have a false sense of feeling great.** Family and friends were shocked to see me sitting up chatting and eating away just hours after my cranium had been cracked open and stitched shut. Give it another 24-48 hours and you will feel like you lost a battle with an 18-wheeler. It's too early for it to have sunk in that you've actually survived brain surgery. That was the easy part—remember you were knocked out for hours. Now comes the hard part—recovering. For some, your face has yet to swell and turn a rainbow of colors, as well as feeling queasy just at the thought of standing up on your own for the first time.

- You'll have a natural desire to view the aftermath. **Try not to ask for a hand mirror or get up on your own to look.** I waited days and when I did, the shock sent me reeling. **Give it time**—it's part of the healing process to arrive at the new you.

- **Don't kid yourself that you'll have days to relax, catch up on sleeping, and reading.** This isn't a Carnival cruise—it's a cranium catastrophe. Leave *The New York Times* crossword at home. Count on being disturbed at least every other hour for vital sign checks, doctors and nurses making their rounds, catheter changes, and incision inspections— it's worse at night when people are *supposed* to sleep.

What to Expect After Brain Surgery Once You're Home

- The slightest noise or light source will disturb you. To this day, I have to watch TV in whisper mode (thankfully Sony has added this feature to their remotes now), and I still have duct tape covering my alarm clock and over the gaps around my bedroom windows.

- Stupid questions. Answer like Bush and people will leave you alone. After all, you are now officially a brain damaged article and should be treated like one.

- You can now wear your own *"I'm a Brain Tumor*

Survivor" badge of courage. I have yet to take mine off. It's a great conversation starter and the look on strangers' faces is priceless when they try to figure out where they took your brain out. Play along—*"Well, I don't have one anymore."* or *"I'm the first artificial brain recipient."* Then pause and pinch their arms—GOTCHA! Works like a charm every time. My local grocery clerk still loads my groceries for me.

- Use the *"brain tumor card"* as much as you can. Great for housecleaning, obligatory family functions, and annoying people who complain while in line at the post office. I always shout back, *"Stop whining. I've had brain surgery. What's your beef?"* This especially comes in handy if you're pulled over for speeding. If you're blonde you can add, *"But officer, I'm blonde AND brain impaired."* Trust me it works.

- A freeing sense of responsibility. If you once had an OCD personality, kiss it good-bye. You suddenly have a greater appreciation for life and living each second of your day to its fullest. Remember, housework is a sign of a life not lived. Who cares about dust bunnies when you are alive? Grab your kids and run to the park and soar on the swings—don't plan it, just adhere to Nike's famous adage.

On a more serious note, I've included a compilation of questions and survival tips I wished I'd had before my first surgery. Thank you to my Meningioma Mommas and Poppas for their contributions.

Questions to Ask Your Neurosurgeon

- Please tell me about (fill in the blank with YOUR tumor diagnosis) in terms I can understand.

- What are my treatment options and the pros and cons of each?

- What treatment do you recommend and why?

- What are the risks and/or side effects, both short and long term, of that treatment?

- If I were your spouse or child, what would you do?

- What if I choose no treatment at this time?

- If having surgery, will you be able to remove the entire tumor, if not, will further treatment be necessary, and what will it be?

- How many types of this surgery have you performed?

- Approximately how long will the surgery last?

- Where will the incision be and how much of my hair will be shaved?

- Expected length of ICU stay?

- Will I have my own room?

- Expected length of hospital stay?

- This is a list of medications and vitamins I am presently taking. Should I continue with them before surgery?

- Is it alright to be using oral contraceptives or hormone replacement therapy?

- And don't forget to bring your complete family medical history, including your own of course, to your pre-op work up.

- Should I donate blood before surgery in case I need a transfusion?

- Is an angiogram or embolization needed, and if so, why?

- May I be prescribed anti-anxiety medication before surgery?

- Will you test my meningioma brain tumor for hormone receptors?

- What medications if any will I have to take after surgery and for how long?

- Which doctor will I see for follow up? Is there more than one doctor involved?

- Will I need to see a neurologist and/or a neuropsychologist?

- Please provide me with clear instructions on how to look after the surgical wounds. What are the warning signs for infection or complications as opposed to normal recovery symptoms?

- How soon after surgery may I travel (in particular flying), resume my previous physical activities, including sex?

- Is it safe to drink alcohol? (An especially important question for those taking AEDs.)

- What are realistic expectations before I return to work and look after my children?

- When can I color my hair again? (I know this sounds vain, but this is one of the most commonly asked questions by our Meningioma Momma members.)

- If having treatment other than surgery (i.e., radiation, chemotherapy, Gamma Knife, CyberKnife) what are your outcome expectations, (i.e., shrinkage or stopping the growth of the tumor, etc.?)

- Is there anything else I can do to improve my treatment outcome?

- How do I obtain copies of my medical reports and MRIs?

- May I talk with any of your patients?

- Who would you recommend for a second opinion regarding my condition?

- How realistic is *Grey's Anatomy*? Will Dr. McDreamy check in on me?

Successful Survival Strategies

1. **Relinquish your A-type and OCD personality.** It is the most liberating feeling, and trust me, once you've been granted a second chance at life, the small things really don't matter.

2. **Delegate, delegate, delegate.** It's too overwhelming to remember all the details you want to do or need to take care of. The only thing you need to remember is to rest, refresh, recharge, rejuvenate, and be good to yourself. You'll be amazed by the number of people (even friends of friends you've never met before) who'll offer to help. Take advantage of their generous offers.

3. **Assign someone to be in charge of everything.** This includes having someone take responsibility for your pets, picking up the mail, and meal delivery. When I first returned home, we had two to three meals arriving daily. It's too much all at once. I quickly learned to ask those that wanted to bring meals to spread them out.

4. **Friendship Saver.** Don't forget to have someone record a message on the answering machine, send emails, or, if you have one, update your website, providing the latest news after surgery and during your recovery. It was too draining to take calls and respond to emails right away. I wanted to thank everybody for their help, but my writing was sloppy and my thought process was slow. A friend of mine offered to keep track of everyone who sent flowers, brought food over, and shoveled the driveway, etc. while another friend wrote thank you notes for me. I can't tell you how much this helped and gave me a sense of relief that I wasn't neglecting anyone who helped in my recovery.

5. **Fine-tune your health.** If you have time before surgery, and barring any physical limitations, get into the best shape possible by exercising and maintaining a healthy diet.

6. **Get a notebook with dividers and pockets.** As an organized person, I found it very frustrating that I didn't have the energy or concentration to keep track of everyday details after surgery. The notebook was great for keeping all the important phone numbers together, a schedule of follow up doctors' appointments, and a place to record questions or concerns I didn't want to forget to ask my doctors.

7. **Bring someone to every doctor's appointment.** It was a relief to know that if I forgot what my doctor's instructions were, a friend had taken notes, which I could review later.

8. **Draw up a meds chart.** I had a hard time remembering when and how many pills I had to take every day. One was three times a day, another was two pills every eight hours—you know what I'm saying. I had a chart drawn up with a box to check off after I'd taken each dose. I promise I'm not normally this anal. Well!

9. **Or buy a watch with multiple alarms** on it to remind you when to take your medications.

10. **Pack a few of your favorite things for the hospital.** Lip balm, scented lotions, comfortable pillows, a stuffed animal, and soothing music.

11. **Day of Surgery Caregiver & Children Kit**. The day of surgery you have the easy part—you're knocked out. However, your loved ones can only pace the floors for so long or digest so much cafeteria food. Have someone bring healthy snacks, puzzles, games and for children— coloring books, markers, and books. During my surgery, Amber had everyone pitch in to make a poster-sized get well card, which I still treasure to this day.

12. **Get active in bed.** (Well, not THAT kind of active just yet!) You'll most likely receive instructions about your physical limitations. In the meantime, ask if you can perform arm and leg exercises and when you're ready, take a walk outside for fresh air. I was also encouraged to walk around the block every day once I was home.

13. **Be good to yourself.** I can't emphasize this enough. One of my girlfriends took me to the mall for a makeover. It gave me the boost I needed. Invest in a few pairs of sweats and pajamas (less fumbling if you avoid clothing with buttons and zippers for a while) and fun slippers to make yourself more comfortable.

    Don't forget simple indulgences like a manicure, your favorite tea or coffee, and bubble baths or whatever tickles your fancy. Once I felt up to it, I often visited a local café that had a fireplace and comfortable couch where I could just sit and feel connected to the real world.

14. **Set your own pace**. Don't feel obligated to play host with all day long visits with well-meaning family members and friends. Conserve what little energy you have.

15. **Remember your caregivers.** They need an outlet too.

Encourage them to go out with friends, get a massage, and escape. When they've had a mental and physical release, they'll have recharged batteries and be better equipped to take care of you. My entire team of caregivers can attest to the following. A special thank you to Lindy for attesting to these points as well.

Useful Caregiving Tips
To Avoid Careening Off Course

1. **Avoid minimizing or discounting your loved one's feelings.** This is especially true if you remind them how lucky they are. Having a brain tumor isn't lucky—winning the lottery is.

2. **Be honest with your feelings.** It's not easy tending to the medicated, moody, mind-altered creatures that we are and we do need to be pulled into line from time to time.

3. **Prepare for the bad days.** Your loved one may be breezing through recovery and then hit that proverbial wall or even seem to backtrack a few miles. Don't worry, it's like that Disneyland Space Mountain ride—with lots of highs and lows, but I can assure you there *is* light at the end of the tunnel.

4. **If your loved one is allergic to any drugs, be vigilant on their behalf in terms of medications being prescribed—** read the chart if you have to. Unfortunately, there are too many stories of patients having serious setbacks because they were wrongly prescribed a drug even when it IS noted on their chart not to. If you're not sure what's in a drug, ask your pharmacist or doctor.

5. **Don't be afraid to ask what is going on or why.** There are no stupid questions and you have a right to know. Follow your gut instinct—if you feel something isn't right with your loved one's recovery, treatment, or care, then it probably isn't. Do something about it—be vocal.

6. **Enlist help.** Caregiving isn't always a choice and like the old McDonald's famous slogan—*You deserve a break today.*
   Apply it to your life.

7. **Schedule down time.** Choose your favorite pick-me-up fix and make time for yourself. If you're not good to yourself, you'll become a slack caregiver or worse, suffer from burnout and wind up a patient yourself.

8. **Rely on your sense of humor to cope.**

9. **Join a support group.** Lindy always says she hit the jackpot when she found Meningioma Mommas. The insights she gained from the members who had been there, done that eased her aunt's fears and made Lindy a better caregiver.

10. **Don't overexert yourself.** Even though the point of caregiving is to relieve burdens, the goal is to gradually return the reins of independence and empowerment back to the patient. Believe me; it isn't always easy to watch our loved ones take care of everything for us.

11. **Make friends with the nursing staff.** Quite often they will tell you more than the doctors. I've been told baskets of Godiva do the trick.

12. **Most importantly, accept that you can never say "it's over—get over it" to a brain tumor survivor.** Once that upstairs furniture has been rearranged, you can't put the easy chair back in quite the same position again. When you tamper with the brain, the cognitive, emotional, and physical healing is an entirely different ball game, often lasting long past extra innings.

13. **Celebrate milestones**. The two of you have come a long way on this overwhelming, angst-filled, momentous journey. Every step deserves recognition.

We've now reached the end and so I leave you with my list of favorite brain tumor resources with contact information. My goal is to ease your transition from brain surgery to the new you.

Cerebral Contacts on the Web

Meningioma Mommas   *meningiomamommas.org*
A unique 24/7 online resource and virtual second family offering support, comfort, friendship and laughter. Committed to finding a cure and proves it by raising meningioma specific research funding every year.

American Brain Tumor Association   *hope.abta.org*
Includes an in-depth overview about brain tumors and what to know before and after surgery.

Brain Science Foundation   *brainsciencefoundation.org*
Founder and meningioma survivor, Steven Haley is committed to finding a cure for meningioma brain tumors.

Brain Tumour Australia   *bta.org.au*
This is a community-based organization devoted to supporting patients, caregivers, family members, and health professionals.

Brain Tumor Foundation   *braintumorfoundation.org*
Guides and supports families during the turbulent times when their lives are touched by a brain tumor.

Brain Tumour Foundation of Canada *btfc.org*
Dedicated to reaching every person in Canada affected by a
brain tumour with support, education, and information, and
to funding brain tumour research.

Brain Tumor Society *tbts.org*
Provides resources for patients, survivors, family, friends and
professionals.

Epilepsy Foundation *efa.org*
An excellent source of epilepsy information.

Meningioma Association, UK *meningiomauk.org*
A United Kingdom support group for those diagnosed with
meningioma.

National Brain Tumor Foundation *braintumor.org*
A resource on various types of brain tumors, support groups,
and upcoming events for patients and their families.

Tug McGraw Foundation *tugmcgraw.com*
Named after the Phillies and New York Mets pitching legend
who lost his life to brain cancer, this foundation raises funding to enhance the lives of children and adults with brain
tumors.

U.S. News & World Report Best Hospitals
*usnews.com/usnews/health/best-hospitals/rankings/
specihqneur.htm* An annual ranking of the best hospitals
for neurology and neurosurgery.

And how could I forget—if this ever crosses David Letterman's
desk...

Liz's Top Ten Brain Tumor Survivor Benefits

10. Meal time is more entertaining when you stick fork tines in your numb face like mine—you can't feel it!

9. My brain was occupied by a roommate, which explains why I wasn't accepted into an Ivy League school.

8. It's a great conversation starter: "I survived a brain tumor."

7. It makes for really cool show and tell. I have an upside-down scar that resembles a question mark along my right ear.

6. I have a legitimate excuse for misplacing my keys, putting milk in the pantry, and forgetting where I parked my car.

5. I'll be on drugs for the rest of my life and am privileged to carry a dog-eared Walgreens frequent RX punch card.

4. I'm on a first name basis with the MRI techs at every hospital in my vicinity.

3. I love to gauge strangers' reactions when I tell them, "I'm blonde; I don't have a brain."

2. I get my kicks when my hairdresser massages my head and sinks his fingers into my burr holes.

1. I'm waiting to get pulled over for speeding so I can say, "But officer, I'm blonde AND brain impaired!"